Immigrants All!!!

By Mario G. Fumarola

Illustrations by Robert Cimbalo

The Ethnic Heritage Studies Center
Utica College
2009

ISBN 978-0-9660363-5-0

Contents

Ring Around the Rosie ... 11

We'll Call Him Tony ... 11
The Arrival ... 15
Rocking Chair ... 20
To the Altar of God ... 25

Pocket Full of Posies ... 27

The Hyphen ... 27
The Bakery Fight ... 32
VJ Day in East Utica, 15th of Aug. '45 ... 46
Uncle Joe's Mistress ... 52
Cinderella and the Amusement Park ... 68
Overture of 1812 ... 76

Ashes... Ashes... ... 79

Based on a True Story ... 79
Going Home ... 87
The Insurance Policy ... 95
Early Morning Flight ... 103
Flight to Boston ... 110
Alma da lasta One-a ... 118
Trampoline ... 126

We All Fall Down ... 132

I Am a Reasonable Man ... 132
The Sinners Among Us ... 139
Zia Minucca ... 145
To the Victors ... 148
The Spoil of the Victors ... 153
Pa's Turn ... 157

Epilogue ... 172

The Gorillas ... 172
The Blue Bird of East Utica ... 174
As Right as Rain ... 178

Glossary of Adages ... 181
From Abruzzi and La Puglia

*... **no one part can be greater than the whole**...*

Preface

This volume is the second by Mario Fumarola published by the Ethnic Heritage Studies Center of Utica College and distributed by the Syracuse University Press. The first, *Wasn't It Only Yesterday* (2007), was a charming and very successful memoir of growing up Italian-American in the rich enclave of East Utica in the 1940's and 50's. Mario, a life-long witty and gifted storyteller, never put pen to paper till he was 70, but here celebrated his love of *La Famiglia* and generally of common humanity in a series of flashbacks full of evocative symbolic detailing. It is a book focused largely on the warmth of family life, centered of course on the women who maintained both family and home.

"Immigrants All," by way of partial contrast, is focused on the world of men of the period and has certainly a darker tonality, of brutality and the breaking of family ties and the family circle of values. Yet always the mind of the brooding main character, Tony, returns to the memories of the piety and love of the woman's world of home and family to counter his moments of doubt or despair, giving the book a tone for which the Italian term *chiaroscuro*-light against dark-is a perfect description.

The first volume has much of a child's wonderment in experiencing a great, vital neighborhood and home life ("ring around the rosie"); the second is a powerful description of a darker world in which "we all fall down," punctuated though throughout by meditations on the consolations and joys of "serving." Both books have the ring of truth.

Eugene Paul Nassar
Prof. Of English Emeritus
Founder Of The Ethnic Heritage
Studies Center

Acknowledgements

I thank The Family, of course, and Bob and Gino
And Don Vincenzo's eldest daughter
And lots and lots of others
And the authors of great books that I have read
And To anyone who is somebody
And To everyone who is nobody

(Because they are only in their thirties, we will call them kids and we therefore acknowledge two kids from Florida who contributed much to the finalization of this work; Anita & Chris. Neither of whom have ever been exposed nor a part of the 'culture ' depicted herein, but possess a burning curiosity to learn and understand. They also believe, as many of us do, *that there is no such thing as bad wine… there is wine and there is vinegar.)*

The Characters

Anna Maria… a tragic and difficult life… few… very few… moments of happiness

Alberino… a baker… a villainous man… too ignorant and self centered to think of anyone but himself… an animal… (un'animale!!!)… he went to Boston and never came back.

Tony Marraffa… a tough man… others made him that way… he had a scar on his face… and he sold fish and poultry

Mr.Aldo Sabitano… a gentleman who worked at the bank… appreciated the value of friendship and education… his children would make East Utica a better place

Mr. Perretta… a banker and a business man… our Tony never knew him… he only heard about him from Ma

John…'the driver'… a man haunted by his deeds on a cold February night long ago, and his wife…

Agatha… who never knew all the reasons why… but understood and loved her husband

Tomaso… the bar keeper… more like you than you'd want to believe

The Package from Yonkers… three men from Yonkers who came and left Utica by train

The Family

Tony... a nobody... now an old man who drinks too much wine and loves to smoke stogie cigars... and through the haze of smoke and wine... remembers

Ma & Pa... Tony's parents... one from Abruzzi... the other La Puglia... the salt of God's good Earth

Salvatore & Angelo... his older brothers... Tony once told his daughter... *If I could work as hard and as long as your Uncle Salvatore... and read and understand as much as your Uncle Angelo... I would really be sumptin!!!*

Uncle Joe & Zia Grazia... a baker... the patriarch of the family in America... whether he wanted to be or not....with past and current indiscretions... Zia Grazia... the matriarch... who could have been a loving and good mother... but was not so blessed... she found refuge in the walls of the church... and the love of money

Uncle Dan & the other Zia Grazia... another baker... a strong man... physically and morally... Zia Grazia the wife and the prefect woman for him

Donetta... Uncle Dan and Zia Grazia's eldest daughter... if Tony had a sister... she could not have loved and cared for him more than his beloved Donetta

Uncle Sarafino & Zia Lucia... Uncle Sarafino... with his stoogies... and his wine making, and his hands of gold... and his temper... loved Zia Lucia as much as any man could or would love his wife

Zia Lucia's Kids... Teresa, Francis, Johnny, Lucy, Carmella, Elvira, Marie Delores, Dee-Bee, Linda, Sammy and Rita... and because they had little growing up, they made each other very rich with their love

Zio Enzo... he died before Ma came to *La Merica*... he passed away with a head full of dreams... and a pocket full of nothing... in a country where he was told... the streets were lined with gold

Uncle Mike... as a youth... cheerful and carefree... in time... serious and philosophical

Zia Minucca... (Aunt Carmella)... a small frail little kitten... who proved to Tony that the greatest among all of us... is the one who serves

Ring Around the Rosie

We'll call him Tony

We will call him Tony. Tony is not his real name, but it fits both the story and the character. Tony is an old man now, and some of the kids might say, "a real old man". He has seen a lot, done a lot… but in his mind never really enough. He wanted to do more, as much, probably, as he wanted to un-do. But, he was never quite sure what it really was or how to do it. He filled his head with wild schemes, dreams, hopes, fears, and he lived a lifetime of them. *Was it wasted???* He didn't know, and he knew, then and there, that he would never know.

Over the long years, he found a haven, a safe little dry spot in a summer downpour, a cerebral utopia, a place of comfort, peace and light. A pretty light blue area surrounded by gray clouds. *It is not what you want that makes you happy, it is what you do with what you have.* It seems he finds much more solace in the practical wisdom of that truism now than earlier in life, and he dwells on it.

However, there was something else that gnawed at him.

Tony recently noticed one of his granddaughters eyeing and studying an object and she… so it seemed to him… gently and quietly, just softly blinked. Tony was awed by her beautiful profile… all his granddaughters were beautiful. *Did ja spect sumptin else from Tony,* something other than total worship and idolization of his grandkids? In the blink of an eye, like touching a computer key, your thoughts can scroll up to yesterday then stop with a page full of words or memories.

But when you scroll down, it suddenly stops at the last sentence or thought. The remainder is blank or maybe unfilled is a better word. These stories and memories of Tony will scroll up and down.

Pg Dn

Since his father passed away, well before he had his twenty-first birthday, Tony always regretted never having experienced the honest wisdom of the man. Was it Mark Twain who said that he was amazed at "how much wiser my father became after I turned twenty-one years"? The second Chianti draws back curtains from his early memories, and now *this old man* realizes, how much he was focused upon himself at that time, and how little into those around him who loved him.

He could have returned some of that love his father gave to him, let alone the kindness and sacrifices his father had laid at his feet. Tony hates it when he gets into these melancholy moods. A self defense mechanism kicks in, and Tony reminds himself... *hey you were just a kid then... just a kid... that's right!* Everybody rebels at authority when young. *You ain't the Lone Ranger you know, and you shouldn't beat yourself up over that. Lots of guys did it, your own kids sometimes; it is part of growing up. Yeah, but...* there is that gnawing feeling, kind of like the shame of a bad memory, its only mission in life is to haunt you, never let you totally forget it, or be totally happy.

A few months after his father's death, Tony recalled overhearing a conversation Ma was having with Donetta regarding the week before Pa passed away. Pa had taken a turn for the worse. His condition was serious... grave. Salvatore picked up Tony at the coffee shop on Bleecker Street, the old Goody Shop. Tony's other brother Angelo was away at the seminary. As soon as Tony saw Salvatore, he knew something serious had happened. Sal made his way back to the booths in the rear of the Goody Shop, looking into the various booths. When he saw Tony, he stopped in his tracks, and just jerked his head to the side and back toward the front door. Tony still remembers the serious expression on his face, and was on his feet even before Sal's head returned to the normal position. Both walked quickly to the door. Sal had double parked out front and had left the engine running. He had left his wife and two little girls at home, because it was late for them to be out. Stepping off the curb, a half step behind his brother, Tony asked a one word question, "Pa?"

Sal just nodded abruptly. "Ma still up there?", meaning the hospital. Sal slipped behind the steering wheel he nodded again. Sal was not a big talker, especially when under stress.

When they got to the hospital, Donetta and Ma told the two brothers that maybe Pa had to have another operation, to correct something or other. The doctors were meeting now and one of them would come out to see them soon. Ma was glad to see her sons, because she didn't know if it would be Doctor Panzone that would meet with the family or one of the other doctors. Doctor Panzone spoke Italian.

But it wasn't Doctor Panzone who came out to the family; it was the American doctor who did the previous surgery. They talked.

Pa had to go under the knife again. They wanted to wait till tomorrow, tomorrow afternoon... and try to get his blood pressure up a little. He is comfortable now, no pain, a little sedated, go say goodnight and come back tomorrow. He's got a fifty- fifty chance. Ma's jet black eyes looked sadder than usual, and Donetta put her right arm around Ma's shoulder. Tony and Sal were clinging to the fifty-fifty statement and anticipated the best results because they knew the strength of the man. They went into the room to say good night. Sal was first..."I'll see ya tomorrow Pa." Tony muttered something inaudible and followed his older brother out of the room.

Donetta sort of supported Ma, as she bent over slightly to kiss Pa goodnight, then she too kissed him and said…"Goodnight Uncle Pete, we'll see you in the morning."

He died the next day. It was a Thursday… so much for the fifty-fifty chances.

What really haunted Tony's memories was when Ma was talking to Donetta well after the funeral, maybe a month or so later… and Tony overheard Ma telling Donetta when they were leaving the hospital room that Wednesday night, Ma said she saw a tear running down Pa's cheek when TONY mumbled his good night. Hai scappata un lacrima… a tear ran out. Did he love his father enough? No, not nearly enough, not then anyway, and he had a lifetime to live with the guilt.

Even today, a zillion years later, the thought or remembrance of those four words can plunge Tony into the deepest, most profound depths of depression and sadness. A zillion years later, a zillion years. *Howdya make up for that, HOW? Well maybe be good to Ma…* what else could he do?

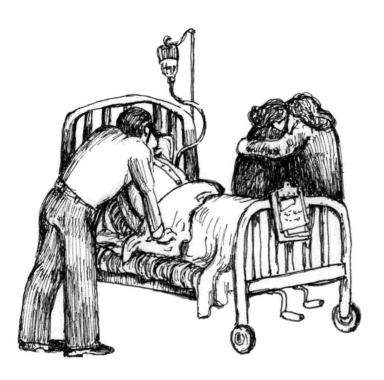

The Arrival

The kids were outside playing, and it was already hot even at eleven a.m. on that Tuesday morning, in July of 1928. Zio Serafino and Zia Lucia were living on the third floor front at 928 Jay Street, between Kossuth and Pellettieri Avenues. In their seven and a half years of marriage they already had five of their eleven children. Miscarriages, still births, did not count, not to the kids anyway! *Whadda dey 'no' bout dings like dat??* Zia Grazia and Donetta were already at Zia Lucia's flat waiting for someone to come there.

Teresa pouted, "Darn!!!" She was almost eight years old and she really, really wanted to go to the Brandegee School playground, but she could not go because she had to watch her stupid sisters and brother and now even her cousin Donetta. "It ain't fair…'snot fair…'snot fair!" Earlier she had stamped her foot angrily, but Zia Lucia would have none of that, and told her to take the kids downstairs and watch them. "Si no…" (if not) she showed the open palm of her right hand, signifying not only a cuff to the ear, but maybe even something worse would come from that little outburst, if she didn't obey. Angie, the ten year old that lived upstairs over the grocery store on the corner, and Tree were going to have so much fun at the playground on the swings, the sand box, and playing jacks. Teresa was very good at jacks… throwing the little ball in the air and scooping up a designated jack before the ball bounced again. They, the playground directors, let you play with those jacks but *you hadda give 'em back.* Someday, she is going to save a lotta money and buy her very own set of jacks and a little rubber ball. "Snot Fair! I really, really wanna go today."

The 'jacks' came in a small wooden box, less than a third of a cigar box inside. The boxes had a wooden lid that slid in the two grooves very close to the top, like a drawer. The lid had a little notch to enable you to hook your fingernail in it and pull. Inside, if you were lucky, you'd find twelve jacks and a pinkish little rubber ball. Smaller than a golf ball, but much bigger than a '*beauty*'or *agate* (playing marbles). The trick was, as Tree always told her sister Frances and cousin Donetta, was to get a good spread when you dumped out the jacks… and then study the lay. Throw the ball up in the air, watch where it'll bounce,

quickly pick up a jack or two or whatever one that was kind of isolated from the group then quickly catch the ball. You only get one bounce! Cup the ball in your hand, toss it again, look, pick-up two jacks this time.

"Got em!!! Good!!!" Now we go for three jacks. Study the lay.

And so it went. Tree's hands could fly, quick as a pinwheel when running and with the wind blowing in your face. But, that little girl Carmella, tormenting the caterpillar with her brother and big sister, that little one would develop a quickness unsurpassed by anyone on the block. Maybe even the world!

Outside, behind the back of the house, near Goomba John's little garden, was a four-foot wooden 'U' shaped fence. The fence served as a property divider and in the far corner, it made a practical trestle to support the string bean plants of Goomba John. None of the kids ever went near the garden… never! The young ones learned early, and the older ones knew that doing damage to the garden would not only mean a beating on the rump, but the *padrone* (landlord) would throw the whole family out of the house. Then where would they go?

The rear porch had a four by four slab of concrete at the bottom of the stoop. The slab made a prefect area for jumping rope, Donetta and Francis were taking turns skipping rope on it. Lucy and Johnny and little Carmella were all near the rain barrel playing with a caterpillar that made an eventually fatal mistake of leaving the sanctuary of his Garden of Eden. They taunted the probably befuddled creature with twigs. Tree idly watched both of the playgroups, and was about to go and join the skippers, when she noticed from her vantage point by the fence, that a car seemed to be slowing down in front of their tenement.

She cocked her head slightly to get a better angle and wondered if it was stopping. It did. Not too many autos stopped on Jay Street in those days, and an almost eight year old girl, with only the curiosity that is instilled in all eight year olds, was going to investigate. She said "Fran, keep an eye on the kids, I'll be right back." Teresa ran between the two houses and noticed that the vehicle did indeed stop and that it was a taxi cab.

The driver's door and the one directly behind him seemed to open at the same time. *Oh!!!!,* she thought, *dat's Goomba Pete!* (A young and strong Goomba Pete, who in years to come would have three sons, Salvatore and Angelo and Tony.) *He came back from Italy.*

She remembered what seemed to her, being almost eight years old, a very long time ago, when Pete became Goomba Pete. He and the *commara*, she could not remember the Godmother's name exactly, baptized little Carmie. And now Carmella was in the back yard poking a twig at a poor harassed caterpillar. And now she talks and even has a mouth full of teeth! Teresa started to run up to Goomba Pete, wanting to welcome him back, but she stopped suddenly.

Goomba Pete had come around the taxi and opened the other door and offered his hand to help a woman getting out of the cab The women looked strikingly familiar, like somebody she should know, but didn't… Poor little Teresa did not know her, but, *she looks like Ma,* and she thought even a little bit like Zia Grazia.

She was pretty, smaller than her mother and aunt, but so very much like them. Her hat was blue, and it had a small veil over her eyes. Her jet black hair was pulled straight back in a bun and in spite of this, you sensed she had thick wavy hair.

The little girl, who was almost eight years at the time, would remember for the remainder of her life how pretty and fragile the woman was. She wore a two piece gray suit with pockets by the waist line and a smaller pocket over her heart. Her shoes were black, and she clutched a black purse. The pockets on the suit jacket had light blue piping across the top of them. Her blouse, buttoned to the neck, was sky blue, and the little girl thought again... *Gee... how pretty she is.*

Goomba Pete helped with the luggage, only two bags, and then paid the cab driver. Teresa came out of her hypnotic trance, turned a hundred and eighty degrees on her heels, and ran down the narrow alley to the back porch, past her playing siblings, and up the two flights of stairs. When she turned the corner to go up the second flight of stairs she started to shout. Her voice echoed a bit in the hallway as she announced "Ma, Ma, Ma... Goomba Pete is back! He's downstairs, Goomba Pete is coming, he's back! There is a pretty lady with him! They are coming upstairs. I know. She is so pretty!"

Zia Lucia and Zia Grazia smiled happily, praised God (Grazia a Dio!!) and His Blessed Mother, and went to the kitchen door to await the arrivals – their new brother-in-law, and their youngest sister, Chiara. They had been preparing food all morning for the arrival.

It was a very festive day for Teresa. Later her pa came home from work early, and Uncle Dan, and later Uncle Mike, and still much later, Uncle Joe and the other Zia Grazia, came to their flat. There was food on the table all day, and the men drank their wine and the women continuously questioned their younger sibling about everything and everyone in the old country. Afterwards, the five men went out onto the third floor back porch, sat on benches and two kitchen chairs, and drank the better part of the gallon of Uncle Serafino's homemade *dago red* wine

When Teresa finally went to bed that night, she on the extreme right of the bed, Frances on the extreme left and Lucy and the baby Carmella in the middle, she was very happy and had not once thought about playing jacks with that little rubber ball. The kids did not lay head to foot in the bed, but east-west; there was more room that way, and furthermore they only had three pillows

The little girl, who was almost eight years old, kept thinking of how petite and pretty her Aunt Chiara was. She fell off to sleep promising herself that she'd be that pretty some day, and sing in an opera house.

Rocking Chair

Pg Dn

Tony was now finding it hard, maybe harder, to get off of that damn sofa. He was sure that his knees were higher than his hips, which forced him to rock to the right and then to the left, and with a Herculean effort, lift his fat ass off of the soft-spongy sofa cushion. This worked only if he could support himself by pushing hard with his arm on one of the sofa's armrests. *Whadda God damn production, just to get up onto your feet!*

He'd piss and moan to anyone who would listen about that lousy couch, that it wasn't worth the powder to blow it to hell! What he needed was a church pew, damn it!! Sumptin solid to push down on and then rock and then, and then stand... Alleluia!!! His son-in-law mentioned that he once saw some pews for sale, in a Pennysaver flyer. One of those old protestant churches must have been renovating, or something, but he hasn't seen them advertised since. Tony told him to keep an eye open for them.

Fairly recently, it just so happens, Tony's daughter was getting into going to auction-antique sales and even an occasional garage sale. On one of those forays into this *new American social experience*, she found and eventually successfully bid on this beautiful old rocking chair. She bid only ten dollars. It was solid braces, back spindles, armrests etc, bowed rockers were all sturdy and well joined. It was varnished with natural grain color and made of oak. Not a bad buy for only ten bucks, but kind of heavy.

In this not so perfect world, you can expect a flaw here and there and this well built rocking chair had just one. But... *what the hell*, his daughter rationalized. *Steve and I could fix that easily, you see it was only ten bucks!* His daughter, with some help, triumphantly packed the rocker into the van, and happily drove home with her prize.

Now you got to understand, and also keep in mind

the way to hell is paved with good intentions. At the time, home was a sprawling ten room house, three of which were on the second floor, three bathrooms, and a powder room, a laundry/mud room, and an attached garage. Oh yeah!...Just one more thing, four kids under the age of seven... and a hard working husband, a physician, who seemed to be on call eight days a week. Her home was a zillion times larger than the five room flat at 912 Catherine Street, with its one light bulb per room. Each bulb hanging from a ceiling chain in the center of the room and each with a strong string to pull whenever you wanted it on or off. Secretly, and deep down in his heart, Tony thanked God for his daughter's way of life and her very good luck in finding a good provider. It may sound primitive, maybe even theatrical, certainly chauvinistic, but Tony was happy that his daughter was in the home tending to their children and her husband leaving the safety of the home to become the provider. To Tony, and because he was from a different time, it is natural.

It may well have been that Tony's daughter unfortunately inherited Tony's *day-dreaming.* *"Make believe – yes I can do that – who sez I can't?? – gimme a shot at it – gunna try anyway"*... attitude, disposition, and mentality. Ma used to say... *"nel testa pui fa tutti"*...in your head you can do everything.

So this solid oak rocking chair was wiped down and brought into the sanctuary and the safety of the home itself (the living room first, eventually the den). When the opportunity presented itself, she and her husband would address that existing flaw and make it, again, the 'center piece' of the living room, or maybe even the master bedroom. Boy, was it heavy!

Pg Up

Those tall windows... on two of the four walls... in Miss Bailey's classroom... Room 5... Miss Bailey droning on about Geological Science... something sinks in. Fresh rains fall from the heavens. Some is absorbed into the soil, some runs into creeks, and then blends into rivers on the long journey to the sea. The palatable fresh water may run over moss covered stones, pass by tired old cities that deposit their runoff from the sewage treatment plants into it, sometimes meandering past recently fertilized fields, always seeking it's own level... *it's own level*. When it arrives, it is carrying the seeds of its own destruction and in time will become part of the non-palatable salty sea. But that is not the end.

In time, the sturdy rocker became more of a toy than chair to the four children, and in their vivid imaginations could make it become what ever they wanted it to be. But, boy, was it heavy. Chiara and Mia would sit in it side by side and look at books. To John, it became the poop deck of his pirate ship. To Anna (the baby) it became a large, heavy, solid wonder to climb, learn and explore. John fell off it twice, and the one and only time little Anna fell off it helped sealed the fate of the rocking chair as a member of the household furniture. It was exiled and doomed into the already overcrowded garage. Boy was it heavy!! And time did not make it any lighter.

When Tony first saw the rocker he was pleasantly surprised and impressed by it, even with its flaw. *The chair was solid, it'll last for a zillion years more. Those armrests are in the perfect position to push down hard upon when you wanna get up; lean forward a bit, weight up front, steady the rockers... push!!!, and you are up!* He used it often when he visited the kids. A few days after the exile of the rocker to its Elba Island, his daughter's garage, Tony and his wife visited the kids again, something was missing.

The sad story unfolded; it is dangerous for the grandkids... *I'll never will find the time to correct that 'flaw'*, and it is out in the garage. The jury is out for final verdict.

"*Do you want it Pops?*" Just two old things, Tony and the rocker... and one of them believes "there is no such thing as junk."

Securely lashed into the bed of his pick-up truck, Tony took the rocking chair to his home and made room for it in his den in front of the television. He placed it within easy reach (left handed) of one of the end tables. *Don't forget the coaster!! There!! a perfect place for chair and coaster... put the wine glass in the center... there... dats good... perfect...naw... don't reach for the remote... you don't need that foolish TV... enjoy the... rock a bit... this is nice... another sip... ain't bad this Chianti... this ain't bad... ain't bad at all... Thank God... it's all good... Hail Mary full of grace...*

The flaw? Yes... the flaw! The end of the armrests on the rocker showed wear, sign of use, and the ravages of time. It showed because they were lighter in color than the remaining parts of the arm rests. There, and in one other place, showed the ugliness of time, rather than the beauty of age of that proud, dignified, solid and heavy oak rocker chair.

As Tony rocked, he recalled a scene from Steinbeck's *Red Pony*. The boy's father had an old horse he was agonizing as to his fate. Glue factory?? Bullet in the head??? Dog food plant??? The rancher thought back to the old nag's glory days and the work she contributed as a strong silent partner in the daily chores of a California ranch. He hated the alternatives swimming in his head. The animal deserved better than that. There was an old itinerate Mexican staying at the ranch, who was either working for keep or something, but everyone knew that he was not going to be a permanent fixture at the ranch. Just passing through. The rancher's son found a beautiful saber and sheath in the Mexican's foot locker. The old wrinkled Mexican may have been a cavalry officer at one time. Who else would have such a fine weapon?

One morning, both the old horse and the wrinkled old Mexican were missing. As Tony recalls it, since it was decades since he read the book, the horse and Mexican were last seen riding off over the crest of a hill. The boy's father said something to the effect of, good riddance to both. But he was, Tony believed, happy for the horse. Tony was happy for both the old Cavalry officer with a saber bouncing on his hip, riding an old horse, who in his old age tried to gallop. In this bitter-sweet melancholy reflection, Tony felt neither the pain of the aged, nor the satisfaction of the strong, but only the awe of the young boy fondling an old war saber.

Tony took another sip. Left-handed he reached over and replaced the wine glass in the center of the coaster on the end table. Then with both right and left hand gripped the ends of the discolored arm rests, and gently rocked, easy like, comfortable, back and forth.

The other flaw in the rocker was a somewhat large discoloration of the chair's finish on the seat, toward its front edge. It obviously came to be as a result of age and time. The urine of the person or persons who sat as Tony now sat, had seeped, dampened and eventually stained and discolored the seat. Tony recalled still another line from the book *One Flew Over the Cuckoo Nest*... a junk yard scene and the author described the junk vehicles as *"bleeding rust into the soil"*.

As the evening progressed and Tony finished the second bottle of wine, he neither felt the pain of his old age, nor the loss of strength he had as a youth, but was only awed by the wonderment of his grandkids, espe-cially when they would giggle. He once saw all four of them giggling away, two on the stained seat, two on the rear rockers. *Kids!!! The joy of my youth!!!*

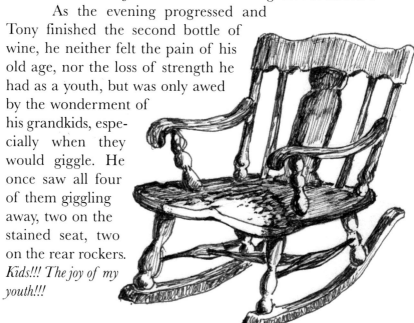

To the Altar of God

I will go to the altar of God… to God the joy of my youth

Pg Dn

Tony, like a lot of us wanted change. Big changes and little changes… but he also wanted to keep the good. Some changes come quietly and others roar in. Sometimes it was wide eyed, running, screaming, fur-faced radicals carrying a fuse lit bomb, but change always came in various increments. When change came, Tony adjusted or rationalized or resisted… *it's not the way I wanted it…* and then wondered if it really made a difference.

Pg Up

The priest and two altar boys came out onto the major altar of the church, through the connecting door of the vestibule. With solemn faces they walked single file, the altar boys leading the fully robed priest who was carrying a gold plated-chalice elaborately covered and properly squared. The satin cover of the chalice had a design on its face side and was as white as snow. The boy leading the procession quickly pulled the bell cord twice.

The small bells pealed loudly, almost angrily. The sound easily reaching the very tops of the organ pipes way up in the back of the church, and then back over to the painting of Christ, with his arms opened, fingers slightly spread, welcoming you.

The mural of Christ dominated the dome of the arch over the major altar. The cord that the boy yanked was attached to a hinged triangular fixture directly above and to the right of the vestibule door. The hinge would allow the fixture to swing freely. The fixture had three fist size bells attached. The cord itself was two inches wide.

The cord was silky and had a embroider design of a green grape vine with disproportionately sized grape leaves and small purple grape clusters. The background was once as white as the wind-driven snow. However, over the years, and especially at or on the area where generations of altar boys tugged at it, it had become soiled and wrinkled.

The cord, the triangular fixture and three bells would nonetheless still announce to the faithful that the Holy Mass was about to start… *hey… dats all right if'n da cord is a little bit dirty and wrinkled… God don't care about dat!!! God wants a brave and pure white soul! and He wants you to believe… we gotta stand now… dere's da priest.*

The procession would stop at the base of the altar, they would all bow and the priest would say, "I will go to the altar of God" and climb the three platform steps, place his chalice upon the altar and then kiss the altar.

The boys would respond, "Ad duem qui laetificat juventutem meam."

They responded in Latin because that was the way they were taught. And besides, some of the bigger kids on the alley stoops, or on the corner, or at the playground, *sez that God only talks Latin.*

Eventually, and Tony didn't remember exactly when, the response (if it is still in use) *changed* to English. Who and what is the joy of our youth? We go to the altar of God, to God the Joy of my youth, *"dem words don't change… dat ain't never gunna change… to God the joy of my youth!"*

Pocket Full of Posies

The Hyphen

Pg Dn

Tony and one of his sons were coming home from Florida, *he had to be home for Easter*, there was never any question about that! It's been too long since he had seen the grandkids. He'd driven to Florida with his wife the week before the Super Bowl and she returned, by air about a week ago. His eldest son had come down and stayed for a week, and his second son flew down the day after Mama went home. He was going to share the "stick" time.

His family didn't want Tony to drive home alone, and as it worked out this year, the trip back was going to be completed in two days, rather than pushing the trip into one day. Two days down, really a day and a half, and two days back, "what the heck, he thought... I'm retired."

The "Big Green", his pick-up had long ago turned over one quarter of a million miles on its odometer. The truck's age and mileage worried the women in his life; he would just fluff off that sort of talk and remind them HE, too, was old and had a "lotta" mileage. These thoughts criss-crossed his mind all the way home, blurry from the monotony of traffic. The traffic in Georgia, it seemed every bridge in Georgia on I-95 was being repaired, the "patience test" over the Woodrow Wilson Bridge in D.C., "people do this every day... ain't they ever gunna end this construction", "watch... watch for the 695 ramp off of I-95 in Baltimore, watch, watch, Shit!!! We missed the fuggin thing."

"Finally onto the 695 by-pass around Baltimore look

for 83 North, here it comes another six miles, that sharp curve, there onto 83 North… charge for Pennsylvania and home." An old man in an old truck, being driven with his son's firm and much younger hands and eyesight… charging home.

"Onto I-83, till route 30 West (Arsenal Road), off of route 30… look sharp for the triple duce (route 222)… route 30 merges with 222 and exits right, big looping curve, you got it… GO!" An old man and an old truck and young firm hands at the wheel and alert eyes watching the road, "Going home… route 222 passes very close to home, it is one of the major roads in the immediate area, that and route 100."

The portion of 222 that they were currently driving on is Amish Country, and near Ephrata. It was about four thirty, and the sun was getting ready to set. A comparatively mild day with clear blue skies overhead. The "Big Green" under sure and steady young hands, accelerated, entered the left lane and smoothly glided by a metallic blue Corvette changing lanes effortlessly, and drifted back again into the right lane.

Sitting comfortably in the passenger seat of the pick up, Tony casually swung his head around and saw the Corvette appear to his front and then to his side and then to his rear. A man with wrap-around sunglasses and what looked like a cashmere sweater, was driving and had slowed down slightly to make a cell phone call. Doing a balancing-bouncing act, looking at the cell phone, punching a number or two, quickly checking the road, doing this act several times, and then, both auto and daredevil drifted out of Tony's sight. He didn't say anything, he just continued to watch route 222 fade away. Ironically, just before the Ephrata Exit, still 36 miles from home, Tony spotted an Amish farmer plowing a field.

The single blade old-fashioned plow was being pulled by three large horses, *Could they be Clydesdales?* They looked big enough, were in a different formation than Tony was accustomed to seeing. The animals were not three abreast, like a Russian Troika, but with one in front of a team of two. Again for some unknown reason, Tony made no comment on that sort of Norman Rockwell scene to his son behind the wheel, but quietly continued to watch the passing scenery.

The drone of the "Big Green" and the early afternoon dusk put Tony into a sort of mesmerized state. He took a sip of his coffee from the cup and carefully replaced it in the cup carrier. The coffee was cold, very cold. It had been purchased at the last gas station about three hours ago. *Good thing it is just about empty!*

Then in a, like a song lyricist once wrote, "blink of a young girl's eyes", his thought pattern changed and he returned to the steel plow and the cell phone. He, hyphenated the two in his mind, steel plow-cell phone, and would neither let go of the image that was now being burnt deep into his memory bank, nor the melancholy mood he was falling into.

Why hyphenate the words? Why? Well maybe because that little Hyphen, that half of a dash, means something bigger and deeper. Does mortar keep bricks together or do they keep them apart? Tony almost said aloud… "Imagine that!" That little dash, that zillionth of a drop from less than a half dram of ink, that infinitesimal little thing could be my life span. When I was born some, maybe a lot, of farmers walked behind horses and turned over the soil. And when the bell tolls for me, and it will eventually, I'll bet the grandkids will all have cell phones in their pockets. These little hand-held instruments can take and send photographs, put those images on a computer monitor and make calls around the world.

It can do almost every thing except maybe walk behind a steel plow. You need two hands to press down hard on the plow handles, you've gotta keep the steel blade deep into the soil. The blade, the horses and you, all have got to cut deep into the crust of the earth. The cutting plow will roll, and then spit clods of dirt to the right and to the left, making the spring planting easier. The magnificent horses strain and pull, the blade remains strong and solid in its cutting, and the plowman tries to steady the bouncing and twisting and jerking plow blade by pressing down hard on the handles and walking slowly behind it. And in their own time, aided by deterioration and oxidation, decomposing and rotting, all three… man, horse and steel plow… will return to a state of inertia…

Pg Up

… The milk wagon was Pete the Milkman's wagon… He gingerly stepped off even before it comes to a full stop, with a thick-gauge wire carrying case in his hand that had eight slots in it, to accommodate glass milk quarts, and sometimes if the delivery was in a tenement house, he would carry two of those heavy wired carriers. In the years to come, Tony would come to appreciate the weight, strength, and the will that motivated Peter the Milkman and other men like him. Did he have a hyphen in his life, something that held everything together, while still keeping everything apart?

The kids in the neighborhood would scurry around looking for a cluster of weeds, sometimes found around big cracks in the concrete, sometimes in the back of the alleyways where tenants planted vegetable gardens. "Per l'amore die Dio…(for the love of God) don't disturb or damage any of the fruit bearing plants." The kids wanted to feed the horse. Tony remembered always looking for long grass and weeds, something you could offer the animal by holding it at the furthest end, then gingerly pulling your hand away after the horse chomped. The milk wagon horse had big, wide, yellow stained teeth. With one chomp he could take your hand off. It frightened many of the kids, but they had to do it, they would be men someday and you gotta learn to do things like that.

Pg Dn

The stimulus that reminded Tony of the milk wagon horse also flashed in his mind to the memory of the horse depositing his dung on Catherine Street, and the steam coming out and off it. Then, old man Balletieri coming out with a shovel and bushel basket.

Tony then wondered, who that guy in the sunglasses and the metallic blue Vette was calling on his cell phone? Was it important or just to brag about his latest golf score? *Naw... he could've been a doctor or something and was making a life and death call to somebody. Ya just don't know, but give him the benefit of doubt.*

Was it this Sunday gospel or one way back that reminded him, the greatest among you is he who serves?

Out there in his back screened-in porch, Tony poured still another glass of the red. His mind drifted all over the place, like smoke from his Tuscany cigar on a windless day. Waters journey to the sea, only to become brackish with salt, and then come back as rain, pure and right. It returns to the earth "as right as rain"! That steaming bushel basket of horse manure that was carefully spread about tomato plants in the shadows of the brownstones, decomposed and returned as an essential or integral part of a fresh tomato for a salad or a Sunday afternoon sauce. It was a long time ago!

Ma used to say, "Those who are not born do not die".

The Bakery Fight

Pg Up

Tony's mother and father were sharing an apartment with Zia Grazia and Uncle Dan. It was on Mary Street, across from the school. Tony's mom had the two boys, Angelo and Salvatore, and Zia Grazia only had Donetta at that time… Mary Frances was to come later. Ma had been in America for five years now, and at that time, Tony wasn't even born. In the summer, Pa was working construction in New Berlin, coming home week-ends only. In the winter he would try to work where and when he could, maybe two days at one of the textile mills, four hours, on Monday and Thursday at Murphy's the Irishman's *"lo- ah- raze"* potato chip factory. He would also put in a couple of early morning hours at Uncle Dan's little bakery. Zia Grazia worked at the Utica Sheets, also known as Mohawk Textile Mills. The old timers and the newly arriving immigrants would learn and slaughter the pronunciation of Mohawk. To this day, old timers, (few if any old-old timers are still around) still chuckle at the way they said Mohawk: *Mo-fork or La moy yocchia.*

Donetta went to school right across the street, and Tony's Ma stayed home to cook and clean and watch her sons. Uncle Dan had rented a small, single story cinder block building that housed a bakery. It had two and a half rooms, the larger for mixing and proofing and stacking of the bread, a small enclosed foyer, to sell to the customers and also to keep the bakery warmer in the winter. With both outside door and inside door open wide… it would be a bit cooler on hot summer nights. And finally, *lo forno*… the oven. Not the heart, but the very soul of any bakery. The oven room was off of the foyer.

The brick oven was fired with raisin sized pieces of rice coal, that would ignite quickly and burn initially with an orange flame …eventually changing to orange-blue, and then finally, only a very hot sky blue flame.

The inferno could make you think of long tongues... flickering and dancing on the oven's ashen gray brick ceiling. They were at one time... in their youth... red bricks. The flames seemed to cling to the oven ceiling and would easily travel the entire length of the interior. The aurora soon ended and the pile of rice became just a shimmering mounded shape that would glow more red than orange. If you looked closely, you might see a blue tongue lick its way out of the inferno and then quickly retreat. Uncle Dan would bank the fire and the tongues that once sleeted and arched across the dome receded. The oven had reached its crowning glory... the apex... the acme, the zenith. The fire in the oven would bake the shaped and molded dough of flour, water, and yeast with her slowly ebbing strength.

No... No... the oven is not the heart of a bakery... it is its very soul... a bit of heaven and a big bit of hell.

Tony's Pa helped with the mixing, kneading and shaping of the bread dough. On one particular, cold February day he had an opportunity to work a full day at the Oneita Knitting Mill... the boss... Harry... told him he could come in at seven... so he left the bakery about 2:00 AM a little bit earlier than normal... that was okay... a good four, four and half hours of sleep. The 6:45 AM whistle would wake him or Ma, and then Pa would rush down to Broad Street and into the world of the dye department down in the bowels of the mill... down with its steaming vapors and odors, with the long drive shaft spinning clockwise, and the leather straps connecting the driving shaft to rotate the rollers of the dyeing machines. The rollers spun counterclockwise. It would be warmer there today with this lousy cold weather we've been having... yes, warmer, plus another full day of work. So far that made two full days this week... and today is only Wednesday.

Ma and Pa were saving for enough money to set up their own apartment. His thoughts that cold February morning: *We'll need a table and only four chairs... go to the Jews on Bleecker Street...maybe we can buy a good set... cheap... you gotta negotiate... maybe four rooms... that's all we need......Goomba Nicolo... recently lost a tenant. It is the right size... too bad no furnace or bathtub... but it is a start... their very own home...* **not a house but a home**. *We can start there and it'll get better.... we have enough for a stove... maybe the old tenant will sell us his if he doesn't need the old one... we got the boys' bed and our bed... yes, soon... soon.* His thoughts, not unlike those of George, Lenny, and Candy in '***Of Mice and Men***,' were warm and good and full of great and wonderful expectations... their *own place.*

Pa with his hands stuffed deep into his pockets of the heavy coat he was wearing hurried along Blandina Street, turned right onto Milgate and would eventually turn left onto Mary Street. Go four city blocks, climb the rear staircase, and into his warm bed with Ma. At the end of the block on Blandina Street, he noticed an automobile. Its engine was running quietly and he saw the two men in the front seat, but missed the two in the rear seat of the sedan. It was a big car... *Cadillac or Packard? must be somebody with a lotta money*, he wondered. Not very often there'd be a vehicle parked on that block, let alone a fancy one with two men seated inside. Tony's father logically surmised that there must have been three men, and the third 'missing' man was 'upstairs' in that tenement house on the corner. A well known putana (prostitute) lived on the third floor. She was alleged to be a comarra of a Mano Nero (Black Hand) chieftain... *Yes...* Pa thought... that would explain the big car and men waiting with the engine running and the heater on. He pushed his hands deeper into his pockets, hunched his wide shoulders up and his thick neck almost disappeared within the coat. He did this to keep what little heat his body generated under his clothing. It... the fancy car ...with its steamed windows... *and they,* the occupants, were none of his business. As they used to say in the old country... *Fatti le fatto tu* (tend to your own business)... He thought only of home and sleep… maybe a good four and half hours.

As he was passing the Packard, he noticed an old army surplus five gallon gas can strapped onto the chrome traveling rack on the back bumper….Pa thought… *it had better be gasoline… if not, it would freeze solid on a night like this !*

Three of the four occupants in the big Packard were, in fact, from the Bronx. The driver was local, and the vehicle belonged to Don Salvatore Salerno. The driver's name was John, and he been instructed earlier by Don Salvatore to pick up a "package" at Union Train Station… that is, the three men occupants now with him in the vehicle. The train came in at 8:45. It was listed as 20:45 on the paper schedule he was given and John was told to do the following; get a five gallon can of gas… tie it on the rear bumper… "make sure you don't spill any… it stinks like hell"…take the "package" to the State Street Restaurant, and make sure the "package" gets a good dinner with wine. After they ate, he was told to kill a couple of hours at the Colonial Burlesque Theater on Bleecker Street. At about one o'clock, he was to take the "package" to that furthest end of Blandina Street. They, the three men from the Bronx, had to do a little business on that part of Blandina. John knew about that pesky little bakery. After the guests completed their business, John was to make sure the "package" got back to Union Station and catch the 6:15 train back to New York, showed as 06:15 on the schedule.

And John… have at least three baseball bats in the Packard… *capircee?* (understand?) All you gotta do is maybe just watch the door and then put the package back on the train. They are pros… they'll know what to do… you'll be home with your wife and kid by seven."

The Packard quietly drove almost the entire length of Blandina from Genesee to near Culver Avenue. It cruised slowly past the little bakery. The double hung window lit up a small portion of side walk, and also revealed two men moving about and working inside. "Shit" said John, "the son of a bitch was supposed to be alone; I think that is his brother in law with him. Whadda we gunna do??"

The Packard cruised down to the far end of the block, and made four consecutive left turns, and John stopped, pulled the emergency brake and turned off the head lights. He left the engine running to keep the vehicle warm. He made a decision. He announced to the "package", "I think that other guy will go home soon. I'm pretty sure he has another shitty part time job. We got a lotta time... Let's wait a little bit over here, and as soon as the other guy leaves, you guys can go to work. Okay??"

No objections from the 'package'... they had eaten a full meal... saw a girly show... and felt a little nap wouldn't be a bad idea..."What time is our train back... six?? We got a lotta time." Two of the three dropped off to sleep almost immediately... but the other nervously chained smoked... he was edgy and didn't know why.

Time slipped by. It was the chain smoker who first spotted Tony's father leaving the bakery, and he quickly stubbed out the cigarette. He watched the man quickly walk by... his hands stuffed deep into his pockets, shoulders hunched up, shrinking his neck into his body... walking quickly in the cold February air... steam coming from his mouth like he was smoking. The smoker reflected... *you poor dumb sap, you won't have this part time bakery job tomorrow..!* He watched Tony's father turn the corner and then woke up his sleeping accompanists. Then both of the men in the back seat snaked out of their heavy coats, picked up the baseball bats and joshed to one another, "...let's go hit a home run....yeah, a home run!!", and they smirked a little bit at their witty analogy.

Pg Dn

A while back, Tony was watching Monday Night Football. During one of the numerous commercials, Bill Lalley of the Dallas Cowboys said something like his grand daddy used to say… "it's not the size of the dog in the fight… it is the size of the fight in the dog." When the meaning of that homespun philosophy sunk into Tony's brain, his first and immediate thoughts were of his mother telling him about that terrible early morning incident way back in time… before he was born.

Uncle Dan was good sized… but so were all the members of the "Package".

Pg Up

… he felt a draft… on his neck and the back of his bare arms, *Did Goomba Pete leave the front door open???… Not like him, I gotta check…* but before that… *make sure the fire in the corner is still red under the black cinders.* The coals were formed into the shape of a dome… *Brr…* he rattled his jowls… *that's cold!* He rested the pole of his server and the wide wooden spread tray (the 'peel') remained closed to his face. He placed the pole end on the ground and stood like a sentinel on guard. He was using the short pole for this side of the oven… the far-end oven which had all ready been filled with the un-cooked bread. He took the Gillette double edge blue razor from his lips… with which all the good Italian bakers used to slit the raw shaped dough before plugging the loaves deep into the inferno… he held it gently between his thumb and his forefinger. *Sun of a gunna itsa fred! (Son of a gun it's cold!)* In both English and Italian.

He finally turned just his head toward the door, "*Che cazza?*" (What the hell??) Uncle Dan then turned his full body toward the open door, the bread server in his left hand and the double edge razor in his right. He dropped the razor and gripped the handle of the bread server with both hands. Three men, two much taller than he, had bats in their hand. There was another about his height, but he looked broader because of his top coat and still another standing at the front door looking toward the street. *Quattro!!* (four)… "Eay che volere??" (Hey whattda ya want?)

The ones with the baseball bats wore no coats or suit jackets, they did however, have shirts and ties on. They all wore hats. Uncle Dan did not recognize any. The one that was his size answered with a Sicilian accent, "Noi veniamo per insigna a te rispetto!" (We have come to teach you respect!!)

Uncle Dan, still looking at the man in the coat, sort of bounced his head slightly trying to interpret the terse message. He then jerked his head to the left, and noticed that one of the big men has lifted his bat about shoulder height, and started to move towards him. The menacing man yelled, "Rispetto per Don Salvatore, stupido!!"

He charged those short five feet… raised the bat… aiming for the left shoulder by the neck… and brought it down with his full force. Uncle Dan, acting on instinct and survival alone, moved the wooden peel of the bread pallet rolled to his left, hunching behind it, then tightened the grip of both his hands on the rod of the pallet, and then turned as far to his right as he could. He did not move his feet. The bat shattered the wide peel in to a thousand pieces… a piece flying very close to Uncle Dan's neck. In reality there was only one sound heard. The bat destroyed the tray and crashed into his shoulder, closer to the outside than to the neck. "Aey Ya Aey ya…!!", Uncle Dan screamed. His arm and maybe his whole left side went dead and limp. The pain was the worst he had ever experienced. His eyes closed so tightly Uncle Dan thought he'd never open them again. His face was distorted and wrinkled… he gasped for air… the pain, the pain! Neither the distorted face… the closing and pressing of his eye lids… nor that lung full of air that followed his scream… none of it relieved the pain. The peel rod slipped slowly out of his hand. He wasn't sure if he was conscious… or even if he was standing… he swayed a little bit… *I am going to fall… I am going to fall!…* he took three or four quick breaths… each getting progressively deeper. *NO… I am not going to fall…*

His left arm... his left side... a mass of pain... with knees semi buckled... his neck swung upward... he gasped... he took more air into his lungs with very deep breaths... and his body rotated to the right. He cradled his left arm with his right and rocked slowly back and forth. *Il Delore!!! il delore!!* (the pain... the pain).... He may have whimpered.

The man in the hat and the overcoat half smiled, and thought..."This is a piece of cake... one slam and this guy is out. Look at him... heaving like a tired horse... his eyes cemented shut. This was a piece of cake!!" He looked at the beaten man, still on his feet, still heaving, hugging his hurt arm, pressing his eye lids shut, barely standing.

The man in the hat and heavy overcoat looked at the bat swinger, he smiled at his nephew (his oldest sister's first son), and the smile conveyed the message... "Good job!" He then looked back at Uncle Dan... still on his feet... still breathing those deep breaths... but his eyes had popped open and then quickly shut again... he is slumping more to the right... *Fall, you bastard* !!!

He looked at his nephew, and with a jerk of his chin gave him the okay to finish the job. The nephew, anxious to please his well connected uncle, welcomed the opportunity to prove how tough he was. He hoisted the bat; half skipped... half danced to Uncle Dan's left, took a bead on his left knee and strengthened his grip on the bat handle. *This is gunna be beautiful... this tough guy who doesn't want to go down is going to be walking around with a limp for the rest of his life.* Again he took careful aim at the knee, and remembered an earlier instruction from a job in Union City, New Jersey... *"not on the knee cap, but a little bit below."* He danced a little bit more, he gripped the bat tighter, dipped his right shoulder a bit... so that the bat head would come in low and splatter the knee.

The other coatless man, not too far from the oven, was watching all this with an indifferent air, a ho hum attitude, holding his baseball bat in his right hand and the head of his bat resting comfortably on top of his right shoe. He was amazed that the baker took a smash that hard and was still on his feet… although he was breathing heavily. But then he noticed something… maybe it wasn't important.

The baker was still leaning way off to his right… holding the wounded left arm… but his eyes were now opened. The baker's right arm slowly dropped away from the left arm, he appeared to slump over even more. His right arm and hand just seemed to dangle. Then the other coat-less man saw the baker make a fist… he noticed he had big hands and long arms. The fist dangled only about ten inches from the floor…. Maybe he was finally going to fall. But no, the fist appeared to get tighter… It somehow reminded him of his father's two pound short handle sledge hammer. The fist swung around in small circles just a few inches form the bakery floor. The other bat holder now noticed that the baker's eyes were now wide open, his nostrils flared, his fist accelerated its circling and twisting gyrations. He sensed it coming! He opened his mouth to warn the other members of the unholy package trio, but no sound came out.

Uncle Dan leaned just a little bit more to the right, dipped slightly and sent that long arm of his, with that con-crete fist flying up over his head, up over the listless left side of his body, smashing and shattering the right side of the tough nephew's face. Every ounce of strength, every muscle and every tendon and every law of physics and velocity were on the end of that arm, in a solid fist, which destroyed the nephew's jaw and check bone. Not on the knee cap… just below it… was his last coherent thought of that cold February night.

The man in the overcoat had never seen another per-son get struck that forcefully. He heard a sickening crunch. At the time and point of contact, he saw his nephew's face change forever. The bat, which was going to make the baker an invalid, flew out of his nephew's hands and bounced off the oven. The uncle looked down and saw both of the nephew's feet had been lifted from the ground. His sister's handsome boy, with a crop of dark curly hair landed on his side, on the bakery floor. On his side... horizontal to the floor, his eyes slowly closed and he lost consciousness. He remained unconscious for a very long time.

The hood from the Bronx came out his hypnotic trance, and moved a bit to the right. He quickly got behind Uncle Dan, jumped and put his arms around his neck. He locked his right hand around his left wrist and squeezed for all he was worth, secretly hoping that the scene he just witnessed would go away for ever and never come back! Uncle Dan twisted and whirled around. The Bronx hood's feet were swinging to the left and to the right... he was not grounded... yet he still held and squeezed harder. He squeezed for dear life. He was like a puppet on a string with his feet and hips flailing about. He still held a death grip around the baker's neck. He squeezed tighter, and kept repeating, almost out loud, "Mother of God, help me... help me!!!"

Finally, the other coatless man also came to his senses. He lifted his bat with both hands... way over his head... his wrists behind his head... (his hair brushed his wrist... he felt it). He was ready and aiming for the baker's injured shoulder... a killer blow was coming to end this surreal madness.

But NO.... NO... not yet...

Tony's Uncle Dan saw and recognized the pending danger. He swung to the far right again, even with the monkey on his back, made that same fist, and hurled that iron fist at the coatless man's chest, striking him just below the neck. The man with his hands behind his head, holding a baseball bat, was suddenly lifted off of the ground and fell directly onto his buttocks. While in a seated position, he blinked and tried very hard to catch his breath. He panted and panted... he could not even bend his neck downward.

The baker was still twisting and turning, trying to get the man with a choke hold off of his back. The look out man, the Utican, who was only supposed to drive and take the "New York Boys" to a show and dinner and back to Union Station… witnessed as the little piece of cake 'job' quickly become a mother's worst nightmare. He retrieved the unconscious nephew's baseball bat from near the oven. Picked it up with two hands, spaced his grip about eighteen inches apart… waist high… and moved to the man with a broken shoulder and the still heavy coated man flapping and waddling in the air… not touching the ground.

Twelve… no fourteen… years ago… this approaching man recalled… as an inductee/recruit… the bayonet drill at Fort Dix… and a fat ass sergeant yelling, "On guard!! Short lunge and hold… Butt stroke and hold… Stick… hold… return… vertical butt stroke hold… slash… kill!!!" The sergeant's responsibilities… those young recruits who were ready to save Democracy for mankind in the spring of 1918… went through the motions like chorus line girls… with their 'ought-three' Springfield's.

He had not thought of that for years… years!… but it came back now and it came back very vividly. *You do it to survive… you gotta do it to survive… I gotta get this bastard off of his feet or he'll kill all of us!! All of us!! Butt stoke and hold… got him… right in the gut… return… vertical butt stroke and hold… got him in the testicles!! He is vomiting and… and… yes he is crumbling!! The bastard is finally down!*

The coated man sat bewildered on the bakery floor, breathing heavy. He slowly surveyed the chaos and wreckage caused by this *dumb bastard*… "it is not the size of the dog in the fight… it is the size of the fight in the dog." He stumbled to his feet, loosened and opened his top coat wide to ventilate his body; he took another deep breath and gained control… not only of himself, but of the situation. He told the driver to go get the gasoline can. Then he went to his nephew and examined his damaged face. His eye had already swollen shut, and some blood was trickling out of the side of his mouth and his right ear. He was out! The uncle called his name quietly... no response... he shook his shoulder slightly... The man stirred a bit..."Thank God he is alive... Hey kid... Hey kid... it's me... it is going to be all right... it's is going to be all right... just take it easy... leave it to me... It's going to be all right." But, the uncle himself wasn't so sure that everything was going to be all right.

Earlier that week Uncle Dan and Aunt Grace, *hai fatti le counti* checked and counted the money they had available. They could have easily afforded ten dollars for five 100 pound sacks of flour, but Mr. Griffith, the flour man, would give him a special price. The offer was ten sacks for seventeen–fifty. They could profit... get further ahead... with a deal like that. Maybe Goomba Pete (Tony's Father) could loan him the seven dollars and fifty cents... Uncle Dan and Aunt Grace agreed... with the way the business was going they could repay the loan, the investment... within a month... even earlier. Goomba Pete who was Donetta's Godfather and brother in law to boot... they would asked him for a loan.

When they were alone, Tony's Pa and Ma discussed the situation and knew that benefits or returns... could be realized. Ma went into the bedroom and pulled open the right side upper dresser drawer. She lifted a small stack of pressed handkerchief's, as well as the still wrapped bar of Cashmere Bouquet soap, it gave scent to the handkerchiefs and she gently then placed them on the dresser top. The removal of the drawer's linen revealed a green Lucky Strike cigarette tin. It once held fifty cigarettes, and made a popular and affordable gift, but now, it was Ma and Pa's treasury box. The tin contained Ma and Pa's savings; they were saving for a dream, their own apartment! She counted out seven dollars and picked out a fifty cent coin from her black genuine, imitation pinch purse she had taken from her apron pocket. She returned all the non monetary goods to their original locale, closed the drawer, returned to kitchen and gave the money to Pa. She whispered to her husband, "We have forty two dollars in the tin."

Pa nodded his awareness of the value of the treasury, but did not answer. He recalled an adage from the old country… "the rich when they want… the poor when they can." He cocked his head slightly and said to himself… "I am rich… I can do it… if *we* needed it… Dan and his wife would not hesitate… benedica!!" (Bless them!)

Uncle Dan and Aunt Grace took advantage of the deal. They bought the flour and it was delivered just that day. And now, Uncle Dan lay on the concrete floor in the bakery, his cheek cooled a bit by concrete. He was fighting hard to stay conscious. *The thought of three… no four men in his bakery… three he never saw… the other just looked vaguely familiar… in his bakery… the middle of the night… his eyes opened… shoes walked by less than a foot from his face. Why??? Who are they… why did they hurt me?*

He smelled his vomit and moved his head a little to the side to avoid the stench… "oowh… it hurts"… he closed his eyes again and forced them open… Why?… *my stomach hurts as much as my shoulder… Why?…* he breathed deeply, but still didn't understand why. He was fighting to remain conscious, but it was becoming more and more difficult. He thought of his little Donetta and his wife and smiled weakly at the mental vision of their beauty. *Why? Why? all this pain…*what beauties his wife and daughter are… *why?*

The second before he lost total consciousness, he smelled gasoline, and he wondered where it came from… *Why??…per la amore de Dio (for the love of God… oooh How my stomach hurts… it this death coming??? Does death smell like gasoline?… little Donetta's beautiful smile…* and then, another little smile again tugged at the corner of his lips when he thought of his daughter's beautiful white teeth and her smile. He lost consciousness.

A bakery… any bakery… should have the warm

satisfying and fulfilling smell of fresh bread baking, not like gasoline, a processed and refined liquid pumped out of the bowels of the Earth… to burn and ignite… push and change.

The two, still able bodied men, took the unconscious nephew to the waiting Packard, laid him in the back seat and packed snow on his face. They went back, got the other, and helped him to the vehicle. He was placed in the back seat too, and helped prop the nephew's head onto to his own lap. The uncle gave him instructions to keep cold snow on his nephew's face.

The uncle and the Utica driver went back into the bakery and proceeded to pour the gasoline over the just delivered twenty sacks of flour. "Hai fatto la jawba!! (the job is done) rough him up and destroy his inventory… that's all… a piece of cake!!"

VJ Day In East Utica 15th of Aug. '45

Pg Dn

> *… Joggers! Assholes with their plastic water bottles… Good pace… steady… better than yours thirty years ago… Are you pissed off at them?? Why… because they buy bottled water??? Buying water almost seems sacrilegious… Why? Because those broads are probably stronger than you are? Certainly in much better shape… because they are wearing $125 -$150 sneakers? …he was 60 years old when he bought his first $100 pair of black, oxford wingtips… it was some kind of coming of age… status achievement… "Hey!! Look At Me!!!" who is a phony baloney now??*

He saw the joggers on the way to daily Mass… part of his Lenten 'duty'…He gives up alcohol for 46 days too…

March 1st, the padre announces one of the parishioners is 102 years old today. A little old lady sitting in the rear of the church stands slowly and acknowledges the heartfelt applause and good wishes… she's is more than 6 months older than Ma would have been.

Pg Up

> … A search for the mortal soul… white as an overnight quiet snow fall… according to the good Franciscan nuns at sister school… Yeah but… but… soon… it is not as dazzling anymore… wheels of trucks and cars… soot from the coal fires in the tenement houses and a zillion pot belly stoves… and the mills… and the people, mostly women… trudging to the textile mills on Broad Street… many of the men still at home… warming themselves as best they could by the kitchen stove… no construction crews working… labor temple will be over crowded by noon… send the boys down into the cellar to get some more coal… only a half a pail… supplement the coal with the grape boxes wood… keep the heat… and the snow was as white as a baby's christening gown…

Those great summer afternoons… on the back patio with Mom… talking… just talking… The Don Camillo books/stories… his conversation with Christ on the cross in the procession… and the incident regarding the funeral of a loyal communist who bought/hired a motorized hearse because he didn't want that old horse… the one that always pulled the village hearse… to stop in front of the old village church… it would not happen… no stopping at church for a loyal comrade.. straight to the cemetery… religion is the opium of the people… that old nag bedecked with plumes on its head was conditioned to stop by the double arched doors… the entrance to the old church… the den of inequity for the opium populace… the new hearse would just pompously glide by the church… yes sir… straight to the cemetery… and don't call it Campo Santo (holy ground) in my presence…. I am (was) a loyal communist!!!

Nobody knows why that new eight cylinder hearse stalled and stopped… Right there!!! In front of the doubled arched doors of the church…

Ma enjoyed that little story and it reminded her of another…

Ma's story of Vasto's pawn broker… "Ma did they have horse drawn hearses in the old county?" "Yeah sure!!! …but only the very rich could afford to have that luxury…"

Ma continued to describe how funerals were conducted in Vasto… and Abruzzi… and elsewhere in the old country…

Tony's mind zoned into another time period and he could see six men carrying a coffin down some steps… out the front door… the cortege snaking its way down alleys and entering the village square… going up the church steps… then leaving the church and carrying the coffin to the Campo Santo.

U ricco quando voglia..u povero quando possa…
(The rich when they want… the poor when
they can)

Again, Ma remembered and mentioned one such horse drawn hearse/funeral of her youth… "Yeah Ma??? Whadda ya remember???" "The horse was shiny black, had black and purple feathers on his head… the pallbearers walked behind the hearse… and the church bell peeled its mournful gong till three in the afternoon" "Wow!!! He must have been very rich!!!" "Yes, very rich." "Who was he ma??? …a relative of the king… a large property owner… did he own a fleet of ships???" "No… he was a pawn broker!!!"

"A pawn broker???" "A pawn broker… very rich… they called him ca-ca tosta!!!" Tony roared and he roared and to this day still smiles when he remembers…"Honest Ma?? Ya sure???" "Yes-sa yes-sa…!!! Ca-ca tosta!!!" "What a nickname for a pawn broker!!! Whadda name… Hard Shit!!"

And Ma is not here anymore… the big smile caused by remembering the pawn broker's nickname… slowly vanished from Tony's face… *Does competition have that much of an impact on you Tony? Three hundred dollar sneakers… bottled water… the artsy fartsy… the beautiful people… are they all better than you?*

Tony knew that some were and some were not, and remembered also

"We are all dust and to dust we shall return…" And, we shall perhaps return on the shoulders of six strong men or in a horse drawn funeral hearse and only be remembered by a not too flattering name…

Pg Up

You were taught…"In the Name of the Father and of the Son and of the HOLY GHOST". Holy Ghost… Lenten gospel… let His Blood be on us and our children. *Seldom, if ever, First place… didn't win too many races… few stars on the spelling test papers*. "Hosanna in the highest… blessed is he who comes in the name of the Lord"…weak… close to death… sitting on an old, yellow kitchen chair in his underwear… his oldest son, with his right hand mangled in an industrial accident, was shaving Pa with his left hand… they are getting ready to go to the hospital… Pa was sick… very sick… but before that, Tony remembered… V-J day August 15th 1945.

  … up the rear stair case… 16 steps… Pa is sick… no, not sick… drunk… the only time Tony ever saw him inebriated… his second oldest helping… Pa apologizing… he was sorry that his son had to help hold him up… keeping him on his feet by placing his arm under his father's left armpit… Pa steadying himself using the banister with the spindles… the third spindle missing since God knows when… his son by his side… they entered the kitchen… past the bathroom door… past the door to stanza vacante… past the Westinghouse refrigerator, proudly purchased in spring of 1941… past Tony and his mother… Ma watching with her sympathetic sad eyes… and into Ma and Pa's bedroom. It was not more than ten paces from the yellow screen door of the tenement to his bed. Pa swayed a bit when his reached over and drew back the covers. He flopped on the bed, face first. His middle son pulled off his shoes, straightened his legs somewhat, and pulled the covers back over him. He left the room. Ma was in still in the kitchen with Tony. Angelo felt a little awkward in addressing his mom at this delicate time, and quietly said (without looking at her directly), "Ma, I'm going back out to the corner, Okay?" "Don't come home late, be back by nine thirty."

  As Angelo left the flat, the yellow clock on the shelf above the kitchen table and between the two windows… with a statuette of a cowboy on a rearing horse…twirling a lariat… the clock gong sounded. It was a quarter after eight. Tony asked, "Ma can I go down to corner too?? I'll be home early, before Angelo." Ma said, "No, I might need you. Go on the balcone (the second floor porch), or stay in the alleyway, Donetta and Francis are outside on the front stoop."

Tony retraced his brother and father's earlier steps, down the sixteen steps and into and down the alleyway. Ma went into the bedroom and pulled off Pa's socks, his trousers and shirt. In and out of consciousness, when through the whiskey induced inebriation Pa would realize what was happening and would apologize profusely.

"I'm sorry… I'm sorry… we bought a bottle of whiskey," he paused and remembered and continued, "Goomba Nicole and Vitucci went partners and bought a bottle… dollar apiece…" he drifted off to sleep for a minute. His wife bent his elbow a bit and pulled his right arm out of his shirt sleeve. He awoke momentarily and said again, "I'm sorry… I'm sorry… I'll go to work tomorrow… I'll be up first whistle… first whistle… I'll go to work… let me sleep a little bit… just a little bit… I'll go… first whistle secura (sure)…partners… bottle of whiskey… finito (finished)… I'll work… let me sleep."

Ma covered him and kissed his forehead.

She remembered she and her sister putting their father to bed after too much wine. But her Pietro was not like that: This was only the second time she had seen him like this in the 15 years they had been married. She knew he felt guilty about spending the money and embarrassing his Angelo. She also knew her husband was at Caporetto in WW I. He had seen a lot, and like her, dreaded the thought of any of their sons going off to war.

She was about to leave the room and remembered something.

She went to the bathroom to get the white enamel painted water basin, it hung from a nail right over the toilet tank. A very practical and functional utility; it had served to soak feet, to soften those annoying and painful corns and bunions, to soak dried baccala (salted cod fish that resembled a grayish white kite), to keep *catalonia* alive for a few more days (they'll be good for Friday with the fish), to wash her support hose (she had two pairs and tried to alternate them daily). It served a zillion beneficial uses.

The basin had a small quarter inch circle on the outside rim to enable a person to hang it. Ma put a broken piece of shoe string… it was black… looped and knotted it in the small punched-out hole… it made it easier to hang up. It also had an inch to an inch and a half gauge in the enamel finish, (near the shoe string loop) a black ugly scar of a long forgotten accident. She took the white enamel painted water basin, along with newspaper sheets of yesterday's paper and quietly re-entered the bedroom. She spread out the paper by the head of the bed, and then placed the basin close to the edge of the bed on the paper. If we have an accident, this may save washing the floor.

Pa stirred and she heard him moan and say, "First whistle… for sure… I'm sorry… I'll go to work… I'll work hard…" He drifted off again. She knew he would. She closed the door quietly and asked herself, "What is there to forgive??" and she answered in a micro-second, "Niente!!" (nothing).

Uncle Joe's Mistress

Alberino was drunk… again. He was standing at the far end of Tomaso's long, mahogany bar, swaying and sort of rocking, muttering to himself. He stumbled a bit when he tried to change his right foot and his left foot on the bar rail; looking like an awkward bird flopping and fluttering on a tree limb. *Steady…. Steady… all right there… steady… too much vino… troppo… ho-kay… you are all right now… another sip… aah!!!*

He mumbled something about working too hard and getting up at the crack of dawn, baking his bread and the lousy cost of rice coal these days. How is he going to get ahead… and… and… another sip. *It is gone!!!*

Tomaso came down to Alberino's perch on his magnificent mahogany bar and asked him if he shouldn't go home now. Alberino almost immediately became defensive, and with an over exaggerated shake of his head… flailing his right arm violently… replied in a fierce angry tone…"Non!! Non!! I want another glass of wine." Steadying himself with his left hand on that magnificent mahogany bar, he wobbled a bit. He reached into his pocket with his right hand and slammed his last twenty-five cent piece on the bar. That was good for at least two more glasses.

Tomaso hesitated for a second, and wondered *how is this drunk going to get home?* He knew he would not, nor could not, do again what he did a week ago. That was to drag, prop, support and almost carry him all the way down the two city blocks to his apartment. Alberino recently leased, less than a year now, an old converted barn; it had a rickety, not too safe, outside staircase with no roof up to the small three room flat in a loft. It housed a bakery at the ground level. The bakery had one small brick oven, maybe eight by ten, small by Tony's Uncle Joe's standards… who now owned two side-by-side, each thirty by almost twenty feet, beautiful brick ovens with facing of white enamel coated bricks on the front for all to see.

"Damn it!!" Tomaso thought, "let him get as spoiled as he wants... if he is here at closing... I'll take him outside and leave him at the curb... like I wanted to last time... I don't care if it is raining out or not!" He vividly remembered that last week he stumbled and almost fell with his human cargo climbing up that rickety exposed staircase.

He picked up Alberino's quarter, went to the center of the bar, put the coin in his Jewish piano. *If he asks for the change, I'll tell him there was none,* he rationalized. He got the wine gallon from the small tub, returned to Alberino's perch and refilled his glass.

Alberino only complained about how long it took, forgetting about the change.

Tony's Uncle Joe walked into the bar, greeted some friends and stationed himself by the cash register, midway on that long magnificent mahogany bar. Tomaso greeted him warmly, and asked how business was going. You see, Uncle Joe and Alberino both operated bakeries within two and half blocks from one another. Uncle Joe's being the more successful of the two. Tomaso, and everyone else, knew that this was due to the fact that Uncle Joe had (in quasi-bondage) use of two strapping teenage bothers, his sister Carmella, and his wife's four younger sisters, ranging in age from sixteen to twenty-four. The four girls worked in the local textile mills, his sister Carmella was housekeeper and cook, and his brothers worked in his bakery and also delivered bread. He and his wife... Zia Grazia la Fornata..., who also worked in the bakery, managed ALL the finances... each and every penny. A responsibility... a dowry for the girls... money for the old country... expense for the business... never enough, but a lot better off than that poor old drunken Alberino, with a young bride 17 years his junior and his little old horse barn converted bakery, and a small and meager apartment in a converted hay loft.

Tomaso asked Uncle Joe about the well being of his charges and/or his 'responsibilities' and especially of his brothers Enzo and Michael. Tomaso liked the boys, but seldom saw them. He enjoyed the youngest, Michael, with his full crop of reddish hair, and quick humor. Enzo was more serious and brooding, but very obedient and hard working. Uncle Joe informed Tomaso that the boys took the truck to Norwich to deliver bread to the bean picking shacks and on the way back, they were going to pick up the road construction crew for a weekend overnight in the city with their families. A reasonable round trip. The fare was charged to the construction crew, and upon Zia Grazia's insistence, an additional three cent surcharge was placed on every loaf of bread delivered to the bean picking shacks.

That old wooden wheeled hard-riding truck earned its keep, and then some. Young Michael was dying to learn how to drive, and going down (only during daylight hours) Enzo made him practice, unbeknownst to their sister-in-law. Uncle Joe continued to tell Tomaso that his wife and the young girls went to a novena at Our Lady of Mount Carmel and his only sister in America (at that time), was washing and pressing clothes for mass tomorrow. Uncle Joe purchased a box of Tuscan cigars, five of them... the long eight inch ones, pulled one out and struck a wooden match from the Blue Diamond match box. He lit it up and his head disappeared in a cloud of blue-grayish smoke. He leaned back a bit from the dark mahogany bar, stepped toward a nearby spittoon, and expectorated into the center of it. *Bull's Eye!*

Chit-chatting with Tomaso, the conversation bounced from finding suitable mates for his four sisters-in-law... one of them already twenty four years old, to the seating arrangement in the bakery truck... when it was used to transport the entire family, excluding Carmella, to the eleven clock mass last Sunday. Tomaso had seen them going down Catherine last Sunday, with Joe and his wife, with her big picture hat, and Enzo, all in the truck open-air cab... the remainder in the truck covered canvas bed. Tomaso thought the oversize hat looked silly and stupid, to him anyway, but he didn't say it to Uncle Joe. Along the same path of delicate discretion, Tomaso thought about the other women in Uncle Joe's household, *The four young girls... happy... quick... buxom... hard working... THEY wouldn't create a problem for him... he'll marry them off soon enough... and if his wife had any to say about the arranged marriages... as she probably will... there'd be a frugal dowry.*

But Carmella, Joe's sister, Tomaso continued to muse, was another story. *She is slow and not too bright... small... sickly... bashful to a fault... Joe is stuck with her... Well, it makes it easier for his wife with a built-in maid, cook, seamstress, laundress, and all around unappreciated slave.* Tomaso sensed that all those in that household treated that poor little woman with disdain... all... except her oldest brother. When in her company, it was easy for all to see and notice how Uncle Joe's eyes softened a bit, and his facial muscles would relax, just a little bit, and a little smile would tug at the edge of his lips. An obligation of protection, understanding and patience... a duty and a promise made at Ellis Island detention center. The young girls would poke fun at Carmella's shortcomings, her younger brothers occasionally showed some disrespect, and Zia Grazia could be harsh and demanding of the small, confused girl. Yes, all this... but never ever in Uncle Joe's presence.

Earlier in the day, before Enzo and Michael made the trip to the bean picking shacks and to the construction site in New Berlin, Uncle Joe told his brothers that since about half of the construction workers wanted to be dropped off at Tomaso's, the boys should go in and meet him there. He promised to buy them a beer or two, even though Michael was too young by American law, but *what the hell!!!* It was only a couple of lousy beers... not whiskey or wine; furthermore the boys liked their beer.

Uncle Joe had a good week, and very early (four o'clock) this Monday morning Enzo and Michael would bring the workers back to the job site. On the way back the boys were to stop at the big Polack's farm at Paris Hill. Waiting for them would be ten hundred pound sacks of potatoes. The potatoes were to go to the Irishman, Murphy, who operated a potato chip factory on the other side of Third Avenue. Uncle Joe and Zia Grazia would get one sack of potatoes 'free' for themselves, plus a dollar each, for delivering the remaining nine. This deal with the Irishman might be good for a couple of months... or at least until the snow would start, and the construction sites closed down.

Yes, Uncle Joe had a very good week!

It was just drizzling when Uncle Joe got to Tomaso's bar, but now it was picking up in volume, big drops that burst on the concrete sidewalks and made rings in the puddles that overlapped one another... and sometimes with a gust of wind driving the rain at an angle, the puddle would look like it was boiling. The rain was taking its revenge and Uncle Joe wondered why. He was looking at a fairly small patch just under the half swinging door of the bar room. He was mesmerized, not blinking, in a hypnotic state, just watching the beating rain trying to punish the concrete sidewalk. He thought of his younger brothers... "They'll be here shortly... it is almost nine o'clock... if something were to happen, the boys had a truck full of construction workers to help if needed." He thought of his father and the last time he saw him, and his eyes filled. He thought of his poor sickly sister and he thought of how his wife bitterly vowed never to make love to him again. He had foolishly admitted to her that a long time ago he had contacted venereal disease. He wished he had not done so. But... two still births... both girls... had to be explained... and he prayed *God forgive me for my past sins.... and my future sins... but I am a man and I have needs... and they are... I know... just animal instincts... but they are needs... forgive me my sin and those that will come... I know... I know... but... I will go to the African brothel tonight... I gotta... over there on Second Ave... rear entrance... upstairs third floor... I am a sinner... I am a man...*

His mind released him from that dark train of thought, and he became cognizant again of the relentless downpour. He half smiled, *I'll get laid tonight and go to mass tomorrow…* he shook his head and thought, *God forgive this foolish hypocrite.* He blinked again and sighed heavily. His wife's angry eyes will always haunt him when he gets into those amorous moods. He told himself not to dwell on the image of the widening eyes showing that shame, disappointment, disgust and hatred. If he let it… it would hurt him deeply. *What is done is done… soccessa…* (it happened)… *a long time ago… when I was much younger… I am therefore a sinner and a man.*

He smirked and thought again… *I had a very good week.* He felt better.

Alberino crashed onto the floor from his perch on the far side of the beautiful mahogany bar. On his fall, he took and broke the glass from which he was drinking. *Son of a bitch,* Tomaso thought, *that bastard doesn't know when to stop drinking… he broke my glass… I am glad I kept that dime from the quarter he gave me earlier… who is going to lug that piece of shit home… the hell with him… I'll just throw him in the alley outside… he deserves it!!!*

"Put that lousy son of bitch out in the alley way… get his ass out of here!!!" Tomaso was angry. Not so much that Alberino passed out, but because Tomaso had seen it coming, from five o'clock that afternoon when he came strutting into his barroom… the one with the long magnificent mahogany bar… slammed four dollars onto the bar, three greenback and one silver dollar coin and ordered a vino… "Duppio!!" (Double). Wasn't it only last week he picked Alberino up off of the floor, and told his cousin Cosmo to watch the bar… and helped… *almost carried that drunk home… it was raining then too… lousy bastard!! Not tonight sweetheart… you can rest your sorry ass in the alleyway!!*

Tomaso's cook and his waiter slipped their arms under Alberino's armpits and lifted. He murmured and struggled a bit, trying to regain his footing somewhat, but fell again. They helped raise him up again in the same manner. Alberino was a comparatively small man, but those that knew him, really knew him, would be the first to tell you how mean and ornery he was. He wobbled… steadied himself with one hand on the bar… looked around with watery eyes that saw nothing. "Get him the hell out!!" shouted Tomaso. No matter how loud the barkeep yelled, you sensed that Alberino did not hear a thing.

Since his four-thirty bath, one of Uncle Joe's major thoughts of the day kept creeping back into plans. By seven o'clock he knew and felt that this thought would materialize and become a reality. Come hell or high water… he was going to Le Africane on Second Street… down that long alley way… past the 'little midget' of a doorman… third floor rear… up the poorly lit staircases… Le Africane!!

Uncle Joe knew where Alberino lived and had his little bakery. It was on the way… w*hat the hell… it is on the way… I wanted to wait until it stopped raining… or the boys come in from New Berlin… looks like it's slacking off… what is it? A block and a half…?? Two blocks at the most!!!* Uncle Joe was ready to make his move. He reached into his pocket, felt for his money clip and pulled it out. He extracted a dollar from it and placed it on Tomaso's 'high altar of lust and sin and drunk-enness and debauchery', and told the barkeep it was for his brothers when they came in. And with a bit more than sarcasm, and with a little smirk, told him if there was any change left over, to give it the boys to take home. He knew with Tomaso, there was never any change, and he smiled to himself because he was certain beyond any shadow of doubt his brothers, especially frisky Michelini ("Little Mike"), would stay there drinking until Tomaso started to ask for money. The boys would challenge his count with their well deflated number. He trained his younger brothers well in the ways of the outside world.

He grabbed Alberino's right arm, twisted it over and around his neck… felt the heft of the newly acquired cargo…

Not bad!! A piece of cake... and started for the door, *drop this off in a couple of blocks... and... then go to Le Africane.* It was still raining, raining just hard enough to dampen his hat and part of his shirt and trousers. Another little smile crossed Uncle Joe's lips as he thought, *well at least Alberino's arm and shoulder is protecting me from some of this rain.*

Alberino's little bakery was, as we know, a converted horse barn with a hip roof that once was a fairly spacious hay loft. The barn and the large two story brick flat roof residency was, at one time owned, by a prosperous Welsh-Irish man who was a coal and ice dealer. Both barn and resident were made of red brick. The Welsh-Irishman had two teams of horses. The barn, which sat way in the back of the property lot, bordered on Broad Street, and had gone through many, many renovations as the city grew with the immigrant influx. The latest for the former, partially brick–frame barn, was a conversion into a bakery, and that four room apartment in the former hay loft.

One ambitious and hard working, a very hard working and frugal Bruzzese, bought the house and barn some 18 years before, and he too, like those before him who resided at that property, also prospered. The Bruzzese amassed his 'fortune' and like he always said he was going to do, returned to Italy and to his beloved and beautiful Pescara on the Adriatic Sea. He lived like a king, and enjoyed his good fortune, until a British war cruiser fired five-inch shells into the country side, and totally destroyed his villa and all the occupants therein. That happened in 1943; well anyway that's the way the story went. He and his wife never had children.

The loft-converted apartment entrance was a frame staircase, attached to an outside wall, and had no cover or canopy. Back when the barn became a first floor bakery, and shortly after the oven was installed, the owner had line put in. A water line. They buried the water line forty eight inches below the surface... no frozen external water pipes for the bakery… not like the main residence, where two years before the incoming line froze and burst underground… costing a bushel basket of money to repair. They not only ran an underground gas line just for cooking, but also an above ground, single wire electrical line. The electrical line came from the residence and was a good ten feet above ground and entered the converted barn at about the loft's floor. Once inside, they split the line, one part downward into the bakery, the other part upward into the flat. The wires neatly traveled on parallel lines, and were kept separated by knob & tube spacers. The wiring was all exposed. It's only intended purpose was to provide lighting.

There were two potbelly stoves. They were identical, one in the bakery, the other upstairs, near the stand where the two-ringed gas jet was set up. The gas jets were salvaged from a house fire a few years back, cleaned and now properly connected. The converted hay loft had a fairly large kitchen, with a wooden rectangular table, five chairs (only two matched), an icebox, and a metal four shelf cupboard… only twenty inches wide and sixty inches high. This metal cupboard was home to four tumblers and three stemmed wine glasses, as well as six plates and five good size (non-cup like) soup bowls. Few, if any matched. That was the second shelf from the top. The top shelf had a half gallon can of Gemma olive oil, various jars of spices, including an old mayonnaise jar filled with oil and garlic, a gallon tin of flour, and a bag of salt.

The third shelf… second from the bottom… had dish cloths, a large table cloth and towels. The dish cloths and table cloth were all made from flour sacks… bleached and scrubbed and bleached and scrubbed and bleached and scrubbed… until the once colorful and picturesque inked printing was gone, or at least well faded. It was always difficult, if not impossible, to get the cloth used to make flour sacks soft.

The bottom shelf housed the large kettle, a cast iron skillet and one gallon of homemade wine. One of Alberino's customers had bartered for ten days worth of free bread in exchange for the 'grape'. The part-time wine maker was… at this point in time… and because Alberino often times asks for advanced extensions for a fresh gallon, guaranteed bread for the next several months.

There were no windows in the loft, necessitating the single pull chain light bulb fixture in the kitchen, and the kitchen only. It was on most of the times. There was a flimsy partition that divided less than two fifths of the total loft area. The entrance to this partitioned area was a three foot opening. It had no door, only a gray curtain, once a blanket, hanging from a rod and it was attached to the rod with twisted one inch rings made from old, scrap electrical wires. However, it did glide smoothly.

It served as the bedroom door. There was, of course, a bed, an ornate brass bed with (a not too thick) straw mattress. There was also a large steamer trunk used to store clothing and bedding. The steamer trunk came to America with Alberino's first wife. It was 'her home'. Alberino's first wife died shortly after they married. And, those that knew her well would tell you she welcomed death with open arms. They never had children.

Also, in the kitchen was a small sink with only one cold water tap near the stove. The sink had a small 15 X 15 inch mirror over it that Alberino would use when he shaved on Saturday nights. His new wife would use it every morning to comb her long hair, and then tie it in bun at the back of her neck at shoulder level. She made the bun secure with three very long bobby pins. The mirror had a crack in the lower right hand corner.

And finally, the door from the exposed outside staircase into the converted hay loft had a large plate glass in its upper half portion. It was a solid "outdoor" door that stuck in damp weather. The former tenant's wife complained so much about it being cold in the winter that the padrone (owner) had an early version of a "mud room" installed. It was really only two panels, which allowed passage into the living area, by going left once you opened the main door. The former tenant had three kids. The protective panels/barrier was only partially effective.

This was Alberino's wife, Ann Maria's, physical new world. Her inner world had remained unchanged, wanting very much to please; constructive criticism and negative criticism seem to cut her very deep. Her size, her childhood, and her earlier and current surroundings, made her deadly afraid of angry people, especially men. She was obedient. When she was fourteen, her older cousin and one of his friends took advantage and had their way with her. When her illiterate and unsympathetic father found out, he beat the girl and even pulled a fist full of hair from her scalp. He even turned violently upon her mother and their son, who tried to intercede on Anna Maria's behalf. He broke his wife's nose and finally… breathlessly… stopped the beatings. That morning he banished the young girl from their primitive home. The girl found a bit of consolation from one of her aunts. They took the "violated maiden" to a convent in the next village, from which a childless couple going to America asked Anna Maria and the Mother Superior of the convent if they'd like to join them and help make a new life in America together. Both agreed.

In time, and facing the challenges of their new surroundings, the aging childless couple from the mountain village blessed and married off their charge to a widow baker, that is Alberino, who was quite a few years older than she was. But, work was scarce, and he was a baker, a tradesman in their eyes, and she was small, but strong and obedient… and a good worker. Anna Maria was much better for him than he was for her, but you have to think of the future, security, and bread on the table.

It happened, it just happened… neither planned it… neither plotted it…neither schemed it… it just happened. Maybe… just maybe, all of Anne Marie's frustrations for the week… the month…the year… came to a head. The numerous disappointments… the latest being that very day… when they were supposed to go and visit a comarri at seven. It would have been the first time Anna Maria was "out visiting" in more than six months. But… no… he took the "extra-saved" money and went to Tomaso's. And, now he is home… *Look at him!!! Flopping face first onto the bed… lying obliquely… sprawled out like a beached whale.*

And the thunder!!!!… The flash of lighting… and then the shattering clap of thunder… it frightened her… it always frightened her. As a child in the mountains of Abruzzi, the thunder would clatter loudly… roll down the valley… bounce off of another mountain and come echoing back as the second flash would appear. The cycle would start again. It frightened her in Naples, when leaving for America, it frightened her at the convent and now it is frightening her again. The flashes, and then the thunder would appear to come straight down from the heavens into the narrow alleys… loud… frightening… another flash… *Oh God Let it stop!!!…*

And then, the explosion of sound. And now here… here in America… the flash and thunder resurrected that old hidden fear… the fear of a little girl in the Abruzzi mountains still remained in the soul of this woman.

She scarcely knew the man who brought her husband home that stormy night, other than he was a baker and owned his own bakery not far away. She has seen his wife mostly at church. His wife was very active in various functions, popular, wise, and respected… and… rich.

…but Uncle Joe, like any other man, had a need… a lust…an animal instinct… and sickness from his past… but worse… an unforgiving wife…

The nose of a dog… the heel of a monk… the ass of a woman…

Uncle Joe quietly said something to her but in her state of frustration and fear, despair and shame, she did not comprehend all of what little was said. She managed to direct him by raising her arm and pointing to the bedroom. She stood frozen by the alcove wall of their apartment's only entrance. Through the grief, and recalling her social obligation when someone shows you an act of kindness, her mind raced as to what token, or gift, she could render this man who helped her husband home. She broke free of her quasi hypnotic state of immobility and went to the pantry... *What??? What?? Can I give him??? I have no money!!* There was a half jar of olive oil in the pantry... her only supply... she grasped it with two hands and returned to the doorway.

Like a child trying to offer thirsty man water, she held the jar with both hands and raised it and vigorously nodded, hoping he would accept the offering. Uncle Joe smiled and nodded no. He said something that neither heard. Uncle Joe looked at the young woman's face and saw she was on the verge of tears. He raised his voice just a half octave higher than the previous mute comment and said... "No, NO!!! Thank you, it is not necessary... che era niente... it was nothing... niente!!!"

It is nobody's fault and everybody's fault.

Anna Maria bowed her head, closed her eyes, nodded a quick acceptance of the refusal, and returned the jar to the pantry. She wrung her hands, and kept them close to her apron bib. She made her way back to the door, and was going to open it and let the kind understanding man out, out into the rain. Uncle Joe was a step behind her. She hoped for his sake that the rain had slackened.

Just when she reached for the door knob, a blinding flash made the apartment as bright as the sun, and almost instantaneously, it was followed by the loudest clap of thunder she had ever heard. She spun around, banged her back to the wall, shut her eyes tightly, and trembled and cried. It frightened her terribly, and then in a panic and a feeling that death was so very near, she screamed and catapulted into Uncle Joe's arms. She was accepted. Still trembling and crying she literally climbed up his body and hooked her neck onto his shoulder. Then, like a child so frightened, that all that was wanted or needed was to return to the safety of her mother's womb.

Uncle Joe, because he too was startled by the flash and the sharp piercing sound, instinctively embraced her, pushed her back into the wall. He felt her breast against his chest and the warmth of her tears, as his cheek laid against hers. He made a slight adjustment, and he hooked his neck over her shoulder and dug his chin into the nape of her neck. She was sobbing and repeating… *o Dio… o Dio… sono*

paura… sono tanto paura!!! (Oh God... Oh God… I am afraid… I am so afraid!!!) The man she clung to spoke softly to her, reassuring her it was nothing only thunder, and soon the storm would pass. She hugged him tighter, hoping and praying it was true. She had never seen a flash that bright nor heard a sound as loud.

He was neither cold nor ill, but some basic instinct deep within him caused his teeth to chatter uncontrollably as if he were feverish.

He fumbled around with his hands and arms, and undid some of his and her clothing… reached in back of her… his hands and arms found the fullness of her body… and lifted her slightly… and penetrated her and… she, because of her state of fear which obliterated every moral and immoral thought she had ever had, was totally oblivious and unaware of his actions or what was happening to her. And Uncle Joe, wide eyed and panting, was responding and surrendering totally to an animalistic urge.

Seconds... minutes... hours… years… who knows??... how much time had passed???... how much??? She clung as hard as she could with both arms locked around his neck… still uncontrollably shaking… frightened. She bit her lower lip and suppressed a thousand sobs. Her chin still hooked, and now digging, into his shoulder.

And soon, neither heard the angry... violently loud rumbling thunder anymore. Her fears seemed to be lessening… slowly ebbing away… now only the soft echo of the thunder reached her ears. Somehow, and she could never explain it, she felt safe. Her eyes were still shut… but not as firmly as before. She stopped sobbing and quieted her breathing. The man who embraced her was strong… as strong as he was gentle.

Gently, like handling a sleeping person or placing a baby in a crib, Uncle Joe dropped her legs slowly, then laid Anna Maria on the floor, and lay quietly next to her. He first gently pushed some hair from near her eyes, and then even more gently, he tried to dry the tears with the ends of his finger tips. He looked into the girl's young and now peaceful face.

She was beautiful, very beautiful to him… an innocent child… he didn't realize or appreciate the simple beauty until just then. It was now… he… who shut his eyes tightly and said… almost inaudibly… *I am sorry… I am sorry… I didn't hurt you did I?? I'm sorry… I didn't want to hurt you… I am sorry…* he took a deep breath but still kept his eyes tightly closed.

It was she, whose eyes were now opened wide... looking first at the four legs of the table where they met the floor… then the icebox drain tray… then up over the icebox to the ceiling… the electric light hanging on a chain with its dirty pull string… over to the exposed rafters… then down to the floor boards and she could see part of the entrance door. She was awake...cognizant of her surroundings and felt safe… but really didn't know why. She was content and her body was at rest.

Never before had she experienced that sort of un-selfish pure 'kindness' Uncle Joe bestowed on her… someone else thinking of only her well being and… someone wanting to please her only… just her... someone else willing to give back. *Never!!! Never!!!* From that moment on, Anna Maria was never afraid of thunder and lighting; no matter how loud or how bright.

Uncle Joe opened his eyes and again looked onto her pretty face, he half smiled, and asked again, if she was all right. She didn't reply but only nodded and smiled just a little bit. They made love again, but this time it was not as urgent or as animalistic as before… they loved as true lovers love.

And then Anna Maria said… "you've got to go now..."

Uncle Joe nodded and said… "yes, I know…"

They would meet and love again.

That night she went to her bed and found that her husband, in his drunken state, had urinated on the mattress and covers. Anna Maria took a pillow and an old winter coat from a hook on the wall and went back into the kitchen. She undressed and cleaned herself. She looked around the kitchen floor and selected a spot to lie down for the night. It was not too far from where she had just made love and she smiled when she nestled her face into the pillow and slept a peaceful sleep.

Cinderella and the Amusement Park

Pg Dn

Tony sat in the glider, rocking gently to and fro. He looked at the bird bath on the other side of the screen. There was some activity today, but not as much as on a normal day. He picked up his wine glass, took a sip and noticed a perfectly circular purple ring stain on the ledge from where he had retrieved it. "Sloppy!" he reprimanded himself aloud. And then, to himself, *Something else to do… gotta clean it while it is still fresh… it'll stain,* and then silently repeated the reprimand, *Sloppy!*

He looked away from the new chore that the wine created, and went back to looking at the bird bath. *Gotta put a drop of pool-a-dina (bleach) in there to keep the water in it from getting too scummy… Humph!! Another job! Screw it!!... I'm gunna finish this bottle of wine and then worry about things to do.* He took another sip and smiled to himself.

Tony waited for some birds to come to the bird bath and hoped that maybe one of those beautiful and magnificent blue jays or a bluebird would come today. He saw two of them earlier in the week in the pear tree. *What the hell is it with my generation… the depression generation… the East Utica mentality, work hard… don't play around too much?? Why should I feel guilty about drinking a lousy glass of beer or sipping some wine? When do we smell the roses?*

Ma sez or used to say, "tu sempre sai dove e' nato… ma nessuno sai dove e' morie!" (You'll always know where you were born but no one knows where they'll die.) Rationalizing his laziness and again sipping the grape, Tony thought, *So!! ...the only real thing I gotta do… is die! I am never gunna know everything… the bleach and purple stain can wait..."*

Pg Up

Skinny and sickly, Carmella was clearing the kitchen table after her American 'family' had eaten their Sunday dinner and started on the fruit and more of the wine. Carmella was slow. The story was as a young teenager, and sometime just before the First World War, she fell into the village well (pozzo), was rescued and pulled out by strong men, one of which had to be carefully lowered into the abyss with a long, long rope around his waist. Carmella, it is said, was never quite the same afterwards. Slower, always somewhat confused and uncertain, and easily frightened. She would react in a quick… startling way… like when you'd surprised or interrupted a distracted kitten… always afraid. She did, however, remain very obedient, very true to her God and His Blessed Mother and helpful. At least, she always tried to be helpful.

Some say she had gotten worse when she came to America with her younger brothers, Michael and Vincenzo. Some of those wise enough, and sensitive enough, may have realized, or at least suspected that this recent obvious visible set-back may have been caused by our sickly little Carmella having to witness her father's rejection at Ellis Island because of an eye infection and his being sent back to Italy.

She thought back on that sad moment.

Oh God help us!! What will happen to all those plans… when and how will Maria Nicola and the other little kids come to America?? What is going to become of us… Michael and Vincenzo, what?? What??? Yes, Yes, yes… there is Guiseppe, the eldest talking to the padrone, and the banker from Utica… Mr. Perretta…. maybe they can make PaPa stay with us and me… please dear God please. It was not to be.

Her last memory of her father was of him putting his arms around her and telling her to be a good girl and help as much as she could. She wept silently, and put her head on his chest, beneath his right shoulder… and her tears dampened her father's heavy black coat. He wept too. He didn't want too, he couldn't help himself.

He struggled and regained his composure. He re-minded Michael and Enzo of their obligation to his eldest

American resident son… for the time being he was their father. He told them he would come back to la Merica. "Watch your sister…"

"Yeah sure Pa… help out… sure Pa… be good boys… yeah Pa…watch your sister."

He told Uncle Joe to be a good father to the young ones. He thanked Mr. Perretta for his time and effort and told them all, as soon as the infection was gone, he would bring the rest of the family over here.

The tired, rejected, old man was now ready to follow the immigration officers and took four steps in the direction he was being lead, he and three others, but he stopped suddenly. He turned and went back to his frightened little kitten and embraced her again and told her he'd be back. He sobbed openly as he left them.

Skinny, sickly little Carmella, with the sorrowful image of her father's departure weighing heavy in her thoughts, started to clear the table. One of Zia Grazia's sisters was told to help by wiping the dishes and another was ordered to put them away. There were many, many things for Carmella still to do; wash dishes and kettles, sweep the floor, strip the sheets on all the beds, put on the fresh ones, heat tubs of hot water to soak the dirty sheets over night. For some reason or other, she liked the smell of bleach… it seemed clean and sanitary to her. They did not use it in Italy.

Uncle Joe finished a banana… he never saw them in the old country… and he really liked both the non-juiciness, less messy to eat, of its soft texture and the unsweetened taste of this *'Mericana'* fruit. A full stomach and a liter of wine made him ready for his afternoon nap. He went to his bedroom, took off his tie and unbuttoned his vest and hung them on the door knob. He sat heavily on the bed and took off his shoes and massaged his right foot for a minute. Then Uncle Joe pulled the suspender straps off of his shoulders, unbuttoned his waist button and his fly, swung his legs up on to the bed and laid back. The bed squeaked loudly, and in less than two minutes he was asleep.

One of the girls helping with the kitchen chores said something funny and they both burst out laughing. Startled by their robust and inconsiderate behavior, her brother was trying to sleep for heaven sakes, Carmella shook her head violently and placed her index finger to her lips in a demand for silence. The young girl who laughed the loudest, stopped immediately but in her initial shock and shame… that quickly turned to anger,… realized that it was only skinny, sickly and stupid Carmella who was telling her what to do. She looked Carmella squarely in the eyes, audibly huffed and threw the dish cloth on a nearby chair. Then, in a theatrical fashion, she stormed out of the kitchen. Her sister, who witnessed the now silent confrontation, placed a stack of dishes, which she was going to put into the cupboard, on the kitchen table and ran out of the kitchen too. *Who did she think she was… telling us what to do.*

Carmella was left alone. There were many, many things for Carmella still to do: wash dishes and kettles, sweep the floor, strip the sheets off of all the beds, put the fresh on, heat tubs of hot water to soak them overnight…

Zia Grazia gathered her brood like a mother hen… as a child she so wanted to be a mother, a true mother, *ma non era la distina sue…* but it was not her destiny. Her father gave her to a man who was an animal… driven, it seemed, solely by lust. God's wrath was upon him and those like him, they became infected with an ugly social handicap. It was Sunday, and of course, her husband went to take his afternoon nap and being a beautiful summer day, she would take all of her charges to Forest Park. It was the third time this summer that she took them there… *America e'belle!!!* (America is beautiful!!!)…

Tony doesn't ever remember going to Forest Park, they tore it down before or during the Second World War. He had only heard the old timers talk about it. It supposedly had a roller coaster, various carnival rides and even a ball park with bleachers. It was located way over on the east side... the other side of Culver Ave., past the Masonic Home, by where they eventually built Chicago Pneumatic Tool Company.

He was told... and he believed it too... that at one time both Ted Williams and even the great Joe Di Maggio played exhibition games there, when baseball stars would barnstorm. *Wow!!... Joe Di Maggio and Ted Williams!!!* Tony sort of half smiled, shook his head and said to himself... *all those people of that era... Ma and Pa... your aunts... your uncles... your older cousins... especially the kids... all those poor hard working bastards... looking forward to a lousy three or four hours at an amusement park... and maybe even dreaming about it... whadda life... whadda life!!!*

Tony picked up his wine glass again, took another sip he did not immediately swallow, but kept the liquid under his tongue and by his lower teeth. He finally swallowed, placed the glass on the table and reached for a Tuscany cigar. With a wooden match he lit it up like an expert, slowly twisting the match back and forth keeping its flame high, with his left hand he did the same with the cigar. Looking down his nose, he watched both the flame and cigar tip soon disappear in bluish gray smoke. He sort of whipped his right hand, extinguished the match and gently dropped it into the ashtray. Pa smoked cigarettes... maybe because his work required him to smoke quickly and not spend too much time lighting up... or... maybe it was because of his army days, where he learned to smoke... or maybe it was...???...whatever... but he didn't smoke cigars. All of Tony's uncles smoked cigars.

Tony tipped his head back, watched the smoke rise,

then separate, lighten in density and then dissipate. He heard the television playing in the family room, right behind him. *Three or four hours of amusement every other week or so… whadda bout you and today's norms???… How many hours of TV… how many hours of movies… of concerts… of CD music… of classical music… of waterbeds… sandy beaches… and sun filled lazy days under a light bluish sky… almost white… of laughter…???…HOW MANY?*

A couple of hours at an amusement park on a Sunday afternoon… in the summer… and if it wasn't too cold… snowmen and snowballs in the winter… if it was too cold.

Pg Up

… They all piled into the bakery truck. Enzo would drive, Zia Grazia in the front seat wearing her large black picture hat sat in the middle, and soon, young Michael came scrambling from around the rear of the vehicle and turned the crank at the front of the truck. Enzo set the mags and throttle, the engine fired up, and he too would jump into the front seat. Michael was Enzo's assistant, and one of the few in the household who knew how to properly secure the truck's tailgate and as well as turn the crank. These were two of his many jobs… working around the truck… and some day he too, like Enzo would drive it, plus he was always a baker like his older brothers.

The last stop on the Eastbound Bleecker Street trolley line was Forest Park. The trolley would stop at the furthest eastern point of the trackline and the motorman and conductor would then reverse all the trolley seat-benches' back rests, facing them toward the west. They would look at their pocket watches. If they had time, they would step off of the trolley, loosen their neckties and have a cigarette.

Enzo drove two short blocks north, made a left onto Bleecker Street, and followed the trolley tracks due east to Forest Park, due east. He had the habit of straddling only one trolley track because he felt it made a smoother ride.

Years and years later, long after they took the trolley cars off of Bleecker Street, Michael, traffic permitting, would always straddle the dividing line for the same reason. Whenever he was accused of being a road hog, he'd reply, "Hey!!! I am only using my half of the road; it just happens that sometimes it is in the middle of the road." That East Utica moxie started a very long time ago and many of its native sons haven't forgotten it.

Enzo would park the bakery truck as close to the main entrance as he could. Most of the time even closer than the trolley stop. Even before the truck came to a complete stop, Michael stepped off of the running board and a second later, he was letting the tailgate down. They had a fairly large wooden grate in the bed of the truck that was used as a stepping stone for the girls. Young Michael quickly muscled the crate in proper position and offered his hand to the first one out of the truck. He helped the rest; *the quicker they all get off, the quicker we get into the amusement park.*

Enzo placed a brick at the front tire and another at the rear, and both bricks under the body of the truck, to keep it from rolling either forward or backward. He slapped his hands together in an attempt to dislodge any grit or dirt, gently rubbed them on his tights to make sure his hands were clean and quickly went to the front of the truck cabin and offered his hand to his sister-in-law as she exited the vehicle. He shut the door and followed her to the rear where Michael and the girls were patiently waiting. En-masse, they all moved to the park entrance gate and walked directly to the ticket booth. The young ones were all beaming, the older girls, in their Sunday's best, maintained a stoic composure trying to imitate their much, much older sister. There were always young men and boys at the park. Enzo was in the rear of the line, two paces behind his brother's wife.

At the ticket booth, they all gathered around Zia Grazia; she opened her black purse and took out her pinch purse. It was heavy with change. A quarter for each of the young ones, fifty cents pieces for the older girls (they were both working at the Mohawk Sheets Mills and brought their paychecks home... unopened every Saturday afternoon). *"Everybody has to be back by six o'clock, we got to go to Benediction. Do not be late!!"*

The last one to receive a coin from the pinch purse was Enzo. Zia Grazia, with thumb and index reached into it and then came back out with a quarter and a dime and gave it to Enzo. Enzo did not say anything, his eyes hooded and he squinted a little. She sensed his alienation and quickly said, "What is the matter with you...?? That's enough!!" Enzo turned his head and saw the older girls arm in arm walking to the midway and he turned back to her. She added, "they **work** and bring home la busta (a pay envelope)".

Enzo clenched his back teeth, stuffed his hands into his pockets and stiffly walked away, thinking to himself, *how heavy is a sack of flour and how hot is the heat from the ovens and pulling and pushing a peel... and... he wondered what is work really supposed to be?*

Overture of 1812

Tony's daughter was finishing up at a junior high school and in the spring of that year, the kids and the school presented a concert. His daughter and her closest friend played the clarinet and were in the school orchestra. The school auditorium was packed that very warm Tuesday evening in mid May, and as luck would have it the air conditioner broke down.

"Hey!!" Tony told his wife, "If the A/C is all we got to worry about, we got no troubles!!!" The hottest international news item at about that time was the Soviet Union's nuclear reactor melt down. On the tube, radio & newspaper, they showed and harped about this radioactive cloud that was forming and would lead you to believe, even if you weren't an alarmist, that it would cross the eleven or so time zones of the USSR, drift across the wide expanses of the Pacific Ocean, over our mighty Rocky Mountains and straight to Tony's beautiful Allentown-Philadelphia suburban fig tree and pear tree. It would rain death and destruction upon all... even those lousy elderberry bugs.

All the while, on its eastward drift, it would be raining and reeking havoc beneath with its deadly radioactive particles. (*Oh my God!! Not another Hiroshima!!*) Tony never liked bad news and what he disliked even more was the exaggeration, hysteria and constant repetition of the same item a hundred times more than was needed for the public to absorb. Those people, and not always in the media... but mostly the media, spread and magnified and seemed to become hysterical about issues (*ya gotta keep dose ratings up!!*) always annoyed Tony. *Hey!!! Ya gotta keep the ratings up... Mother Teresa... or a stay at home mom... protecting and loving and teaching their children... nah... nah... dem guys... dey don't sell!!! Princess Di or Monica Lewinsky or Elizabeth Taylor... dat's da ticket!*

Il vucca... la venu... E'quelli che non sa niente. (The wind... the mouth... and those know nothing.) *I hear ya*

Ma… I hear ya!!

The Soviet engineers were not as good as 'others'. Their scientists; too ambitious, their projects; too risky, too envious of their international counterparts. Their employees at the nuclear plant, probably just converted from transplanted potato farmers, who should have stayed on the farm bending their aching backs, digging and picking food for others to eat. *Look how professionally we handled Three Mile Island a few years back. No deaths… no death cloud… yes, very professionally… and… very lucky.*

How good can a bunch of sixth and seven and eight grade kids actually perform a musical concert in a warm and crowded auditorium? What do you want to put into the word 'good'? Talent… bravery… concentration… determination… Michaelangelo did his *Pieta* at age 22… and the world is still awed by all his works… Mozart memorized secret Vatican chants after only hearing them once and wrote it out for his father. At the time, he was just a little bit older (maybe not) than those kids playing their hearts out on a hot evening in a crowded auditorium.

The thought occurred to Tony… *maybe 'good' is the best you can do… no more… no less.*

The music teacher, conductor of the school orchestra, selected several pieces for the performance and made the decision to close with the Overture of 1812. "Maybe he got the idea from the Boston Pops?" Tony didn't know, so, he shrugged his shoulders slightly and waited. It was one of Tony's favorites.

As the teacher/conductor raised his baton, and the kids readied their instruments Tony thought to himself, *this is a tough piece for such a young group.* And added, *I hope they (we) do good.*

Tony has many times heard the Overture, on TV, on CDs… on the radio, but he never again heard it as meaningful as he heard it that night in a crowded, hot auditorium. Sure, it was crude… the kids had cow bells or something like an old fashioned school marm hand bell, for Tchaikovsky church bells and a couple of firecrackers popping in a metal garbage can for Napoleon's artillery falling on the streets of Moscow, but somehow you knew the kids where doing their best.

The current events of the time, drifted across Tony's mind that evening. Sure the

Soviet Russians were fearful and they knew the danger of a radioactive melt down…. but many… many brave men and women went into the fray… as did the Russian troops defending Moscow in 1812. At first the roar of artillery overwhelms the faintness of the Moscow church bells, but the bells persist and then overcome the sound of the artillery. The tolling of church bell is for goodness and hope. God bless the brave people that have hope.

The kids did good that night…. real good.

Ashes... Ashes...

Based on a True Story

Pg Dn

It was late June and Tony had already pulled his garlic 'crop.' He plants at least one hundred cloves every fall just before Thanksgiving, after winterizing the fig tree, and was now in the process of dutifully harvesting them as old Don Vincenzo taught him.

You gotta pull 'em carefully... shake the dirt out of the whisker hairs on the bottom of the bulb... lay the bulb gently on grass... make sure it is in the ombra (shade)... handle each of dem like the nipple of a woman... don't bruise 'em... turn 'em over once or twice... you wanna dem to air dry all around. DO NOT FORGET!!!... take 'em in the shed at night... the nebbia (fog/dew) will spoil them later on... if it is raining... leave 'em in the shed... ma (but) keepa the shed doors open... en a cupa la ayes (in a couple of days)... un settemana (a week) you braid them... nice... just tree he showed Tony his thumb, his index finger and his middle fingers... like they do in Italy... *nice-a buncha... like dis-a.*

Tony was starting the final stage. He liked this part and knew he was going to enjoy the afternoon. He had already muscled the old picnic table and only one of the benches into the shade of the big maple and by the bird-bath. He tenderly placed his entire garlic crop on the picnic table; brought out his wine and wine glass, his cigars and a full box of wooden matches (*you need a lotta matches to keep the stogies alive*).

It was a beautiful day.

Was it last year... or the year before..???... when his daughter came out into the back yard, when he was doing exactly what he was now doing.... and she said.... "Oh my God dad… what are you doing?… posing for a Sicilian travel agency poster? or What???" Tony smiled broadly at the memory and the comment.

He inhaled the freshness of the crop spread out upon the old, old picnic table, took a sip of the grape and lit up his stogie cigar. He cocked his head slightly to the right to let the bluish-gray cigar smoke drift upward and away from his eyes. It was then that he recalled that Tony Marraffa's wife used to braid and sell garlic in the old fish market, but she braided her strands much longer.

Pg Up

Ma was talking to Zia Lucia. They were talking about the Marraffa's on the corner. Ma sez, based on a story about Tony Marraffa and Marraffa's Fish and Poultry market. this really happened!!! *E'vero!!!... (it is true!!)*

Tony Marraffa and his wife ran Marraffa's Fish and Poultry Market on the southwest corner of Kossuth Ave. and Catherine St.… during the thirties, the forties and the fifties… and even into the sixties. It was a squat, broad-shoulder frame structure with the entrance to the fish-poultry store on a diagonal line touching both the Kossuth Ave. sidewalk and the Catherine St. sidewalk. Walking west on the Catherine St. side on the way to Brandegee School was a door to Tony M's apartment, a double window for his kitchen. Our Tony believed this, because sometimes you could catch a glimpse through the Venetian blinds slats when you walked by, and you could see parts of a table and chairs… but he was never in the apartment. The apartment also had a door that opened into the store.

Along the same wall and a bit further down, just before you got to the alley between Marraffa and the three story frame tenement where Buster Convertino used to live, was a double door garage. Once, there were two large hinged doors that swung outward and onto the sidewalk almost reaching the curb, but in time, it became an overhead door.

Tony Marraffa would get his chicken and turkey deliveries at that door. It opened into a quasi courtyard.

The chicken crates were square, maybe three feet by three feet… maybe even more. On delivery day, they were always packed with squawking, cackling white chickens. They didn't smell too nice. On those delivery dates it seemed there were always little white feathers floating around; in the summer it would remind you of snow flakes.

The fish were delivered at, and through, the front door. A truck came from Boston on late Wednesday or early Thursday and after the delivery, either headed for Syracuse or back to Boston. The fish truck was once green and it could remind you of the green Railroad Express trucks you always saw at Union Station, but it wasn't like them, just green and big like them. Tony M. sold a "lotta" fish and chickens from that location. However at one time in the old days, young Tony has been told, Tony M. had a push cart and hawked his wares from it. His wife watched the fish market.

Before Tony was born, so the story goes, "la Mano Nero" (the Black Hand) wanted to share in Mr. Marraffa's profits, but he did not want or need a partner. So on one particular day, some men overturned his push cart and one slashed Tony's face with a razor. It happened on the corner of Elizabeth St. and Kossuth Ave. Young Tony didn't know how true that story was, but he did know, however, that Tony had a three inch scar on his face, between his nose and his left ear. Later, much later in life, another story about Mr. Marraffa came to light… also *Based on a True Story.*" That part of the story goes this way…

Tony nickname in the neighborhood was "*Papa de Porco*" (Pope of the Pigs). He did not like that handle and the kids always made sure not to use it in his presence. *My God!!! the man had a scar on his face; how tough and mean can a guy like that be??… and he ain't pretty!!!* That 'later in life story' revealed that Tony Marraffa squealed, "ratting" on those who always wanted a "commission" from his hard work. The Black

Hand supposedly circulated that unholy nickname, to tarnish Tony's reputation and instill fear and obedience in the populace… *no matter… but that scar was real!!!*

What we do know is that Mr. Marraffa had a nasty scar on his face and an unattractive nickname. But just by living in the neighborhood, you learned a little bit more.

Tony Marraffa was short and squatty. He was kind of like his store, one story high but wider than any other structure on the block. Young Tony remembered Mr. Marraffa would wear several layers of sweaters, a long white apron, and at times, black rubber boots, which, because of his stature, seemed to go past his kneecaps. He always wore a meat packer's white coat and a golf hat. Come to think of it, only a few of us kids knew for sure if he was bald.

The chickens were always killed 'fresh'. Customers either came into the store… picked out the bird from one of the crates out on the sidewalk, then waited, or returned later the same day. Separated and parted, like the state and religion, the fish and chickens were always kept separated in those ice tubs. During business hours, both laid on cold… very cold… chunks of ice… and at closing time the fish were stored in the cooler… and the chicken in someone's kitchen or pot. Should a dressed chicken not be picked up, Tony would send 'Jap' Grande or Tony Greco (his adopted grandson… we called him Greek) to the customer's flat. Their mission was, one, to remind the customer if they had forgotten, or, two, to get the money for the bird, go back, pick it up and deliver. (Jap told little Tony sometimes he'd get a couple of pennies for doing that… one time even a *ten-cent dime !!).*

His original walk-in cooler (mainly for the fish) was chilled by ice. However, after periodical and intermittent partial lease agreements (for a while to the Tomasino Trevisani grocery store), the ice cooler eventually became a refrigerated cooler.

The ice wagon… later the ice truck… would make

its rounds in the neighborhood. To us kids, it always seemed to start at Tony's Fish Market, and it was packed with those big blocks of one hundred… fifty… twenty-five pounds of ice; and covered with a damp canvas tarp. After a sizable delivery at Marraffa's, it would then go down the 900 block of Catherine Street. The ice man… his name was Charlie, and he was Syrian or Lebanese… would go down the street looking at porch posts and windows of the brownstone tenements and other houses, seeking out those orange cardboard cards. These cards… approximately nine by twelve inches had two large numbers on them: twenty-five and fifty. The large numbers, each occupying half of the card, were the reverse of one another, therefore when you were able to clearly read 'fifty'; the 'twenty five' was upside down and visa-versa. If the customer wanted ice that day, the orange card was prominently shown. The cards were tied, using pieces of string from previous purchases at the grocery stores, to the porch post on the second or third floor, or were placed in a window that faced out onto the street for Charlie to read and deliver if necessary!

Charlie came to the neighborhood on Mondays and Wednesdays and sometimes on Saturday mornings in July and August. The hundred and the fifty pound blocks of ice had a seam in them. Charlie had a well worn leather sheath on his right hip that held an ice pick. The ice pick had a wooden grip with the inscription 'Utica Ice and Coal Co.' He would read the cards, then muscle and jockey those large slabs of ice to the tailgate of the wagon or truck, reach for his ice pick and quickly and violently stab the seam. The block would immediately separate… always… and always on the first stab. He would return his ice pick, place a chamois his shoulder and get his ice tongs. With his strong hands and arms he'd open and quickly close the tines of the big ice tongs into the block, firmly implanting them into the ice, and like an animal in a steel trap, the block of ice was trapped. He'd give a little grunt, raise his burden to his shoulder and

Charlie would extend his free arm until it was parallel to the ground and would step down off of the rear elevated platform of the truck and make his delivery. Sometimes he had to carry a block of dripping ice down an alley and up a stoop, up two or three flights of stairs. That man worked for his money!

At the corner of Pellettieri Ave. and Catherine, after he was done with the John Blaze brownstone, he'd retrieve two large zinc tubs which hung over the gun walls of the vehicle. He now had room in the bed of the vehicle. He'd split a hundred pound block and place each half into the zinc tubs. With a grim look on his face and squinting eyes and with a proficient staccato action he would attack the block with piston like force with his ice pick. The blocks would soon shatter.

Sometimes, he would notice us kids watching him and he would throw us each a little chunk of ice to suck on. He threw it underhand because it was easier for us to catch and even if you missed, all you had to do was pick it up, shake it a bit and the chunk would wash itself. We liked Charlie, and we believed he liked us kids too.

He was prepping his next delivery to Joe's Restaurant. The chopped ice was for the tap beer coils in the bar room. The remainder of the delivery went down into Joe's gold mine, the basement where the kegs of beer were stored and where the oven was located. He would first deliver the blocks through an angular trap door that opened out onto the street, Pellettier Ave. side. Then, Charlie would bring in the tubs of crushed ice through the front door. Either he or Dominick or Joe, would remove the grate over the coil system and Charlie would dump the ice into it. They had a half of an old broom stick to help shake the ice down into the ice reservoir for the beer coils. Joe or Dominick would always offer Charlie a cold beer. Charlie would nod and accept it. That was Charlie and Dominick and Goomba Joe.

Tony Marraffa was not really much different but to the kids he certainly was!!

To us kids, he appeared grumpy and serious, pre-occupied, shifty, and he had those piercing and squinting jet black eyes. He shaved only on Fridays and Sundays, when he went to Mass; even if we saw him in church he would frighten us and we'd look away... *he had that scar you know!!!*

Nevertheless, we kids would love to look through those big glass plates that ran up the Kossuth Avenue side of the store... especially on Thursday and Friday nights and Saturday mornings. Tony had square bins or tubs (...big... really big... about six feet by four feet and a foot deep right under the plate glass windows) which were neatly lined with various fishes... heads and fins and everything!!!... all packed on ice. *Look at that one!!! Betcha even a shark couldn't eat him in one bite!!!* In November, he would use one of the bins to display very large 'dressed' turkeys that customers ordered... some of them were a zillion pounds.

Ever since young Tony knew Mr. Marraffa, he always had dogs, real big dogs. German Shepard, Belgian Police, orange colored Chows with purple tongues, like your tongue gets when you have red wine. Anyone of them could easily crash right through the screen doors he had on both sides of his short, squat store. During the day, when the dogs where kept in the back courtyard, you could hear them bark occasionally. But... at night, you could not only see them roaming around in the closed fish market (Tony kept a small 40 watt light bulb on near the center of the store), but you could hear them barking and almost warning us kids *you better not come in or we'll eat you alive!!*

Mr. Marraffa always had at least three dogs. He was never burglarized. He also had a large Colt 45 caliber automatic pistol. He kept it in one of the drawers by the cash register. Later in life, young Tony learned that this weapon was designed by the government for fighting insurgents in the

Philippines. It is and was powerful, very powerful, especially at short range. The intent was to knock charging rebels off of their feet in the jungles of the South Pacific. Few, if any, saw the weapon, although his kind of adopted grandson and Jap Grande told young Tony that they had seen it more than once. The gun and the dogs and the scar only added to the mystique of the man.

Pg Dn

Before he started braiding the garlic, Tony selected some of the biggest and healthiest looking bulbs and broke out the cloves. He counted one hundred and six and placed the cloves in three brown paper bags, the kind he used when he took his lunch to school, folded and sealed the open end by creasing it several times and placed the bags in the rear of the crisper drawers of the garage refrigerator. They were for this Fall's planting.

During the course of that warm June afternoon, Tony finished his garlic braiding… and… his wine… and… his two cigars… and… his box of wooden matches.

He wondered how many times he, his brothers, cousins and friends… like Jack Del Monte and Pat Caputo and Buster Convertino and Nunzio Melchorrie… walked past Marraffa's Fish Market… which was not too far from Brandegee School.

Going Home

Govanni De Spirito and his eldest son Guiseppe were going back to Italy. They had worked in the coal mines of West Virginia for almost ten years now, ever since coming to America. They scrimped and saved and now had one thousand, one hundred and sixty-five dollars. *Rich!!! One thousand American dollars!!! Rich!!! We are rich!!!* They gave the thousand dollars to Mr. Perretta's bank, and for twenty-five dollars, Signoro Perretta would guarantee that the money would be waiting at la Banca Nationale in Chieti. It would be waiting safe and sound for them in the old Country; Mr. Perretta could be trusted…

Why!! Of course… everybody knows he and his entire family attend the eleven o'clock Mass every Sunday morning and sit in the very first pew and he always puts green bills in the basket at the collection. One more thing, Mr. Perretta was not a greedy man, but more importantly, he was rich enough not to steal.

We will go home and live like a king… and young Guiseppe… almost twenty-seven… thought… maybe I'll marry… raise kids… and if I have to… I'll come back to La Merica make more money and go back to Italia again… I am young… I am strong… I can work hard… lottsa kids…

The De Spirito family lived in the same Adriatic village as Uncle Joe and Zia Grazia. Their families knew each other very well. Zia Grazia's father and Govanni De Spirito owned a small boat together and shared the gains earned in each catch. When Govanni came to America, Zia Grazia's father purchased his share of the boat and fished alone for a while, or at least until his youngest son was able to help, at the tender old age of eight.

A year or so earlier, when Uncle Joe found out that the De Spirito's were planning on going back to the old country, he recognized an opportunity and he seized the moment. Uncle Joe never once forgot that Carmella was not happy in America, and was so homesick that it could and often did, make her sick. But she never would complain. The plan was that De Spirito would escort and chaperone Carmella home, at no expense to Uncle Joe and Zia Grazia, other than steerage cost. The arrangement suited Zia Grazia, although she fretted a bit about the steerage cost. She came to realize that it was really to her advantage not only financially, but for everybody's well being and state of mind... but mostly financially. She had, more than three years ago, placed Carmella in her imaginary "worry box" and prepared for the dismal inevitable, which became even more dismal after Doctor Rossi's gloomy analysis of Carmella's well being.

But now... now... with these heaven sent arrangements... Carmella's burial cost would be borne in Italy and not in her house. With the insurance policy and the forthcoming reduction in current expenses, like that poor girl ate all that much and cost so much to maintain, Zia Grazia anticipated and appreciated the win-win situation.

It was Sunday and that very next Tuesday, Govanni, his son and Carmella would catch the early train, the 6:15am, to New York City and go back to the old country. Enzo would have Carmella and her small suitcase and be at their door at a quarter to six on that morning with the truck. Father and son would ride in the cab and Carmella could sit on the floor of the truck bed with all the luggage. That morning, however, Enzo made it a point to have Carmella remain in the cab of the truck. "Ahey, Pepe... you don't mind jumping in the back of the truck do you??? It's kind of hard for Carmella to get up that high..." "Sure!! Sure!! No problemo!!! No trouble, neinete!!!"

Uncle Joe made a point earlier of not telling his fragile sister of the overall plans. When she was finally advised she was so excited and happy she hardly slept for more than four hours a night, saying a river... a Niagara... of Hail Mary's, and thanking God for this beautiful gift and... suddenly... it became very easy for her to smile. Strangely... it was only Uncle Joe and Enzo who noticed the later change, but neither mentioned it aloud, and they themselves were very happy for the girl.

Uncle Joe and Zia Grazia graciously invited the departing De Spiritos and their sister's family over for a huge dinner that Sunday. A great and bountiful table was prepared and the food devoured with the gusto only a contented and happy party could generate. Stories of America and Italy were exchanged by the adults and absorbed by the young. Zia Grazia beamed with an inner, secret pride when Govanni told of how her father was always specially chosen by the pastor in Italy, once even requested by a visiting bishop, to carry that long three meter shaft with the gold crucifix at the top. Because of her father's stature, so very tall, broad in the shoulders, so very handsome, with a neatly trimmed mustache, and that long shaft, the crucifix floated above all and was so close to the clouds.

It was her father who led the procession from the church steps. Down the narrow streets, past the statue of Gabriel Rossetti, and then through the village square past the babbling fountain and down the steep road to the sandy beaches for the Benediction and the blessing of the fishing boats... *le barce.* It was her father... tall and handsome... leading the acolytes, the brown robed choir boys, the seminarians, the priest... the four posted canopy with its blood red and gold carpet kept high above the pastor as he carried the sacred Host in its spectacular gold sun burst encasement... her father. Her father, whom they all followed. For a magic moment she, Zia Grazia, was transported back in time to one of her most memorable moments. Inside she was so happy... so very, very happy and so proud... so very, very proud... oh how she loved her father... oh how she wanted a son to be like him... that tall mustached and handsome man... a crop of black curly hair... solid, majestic. *Oh if I only had a son... a son... just one child... oh how happy I would be... I would be happy forever... always happy... if I only had a child!!!*

Tony remembered reading a Don Camillo adventure, in which Don Camillo was somehow forced or coerced into carrying the Crucifix on a long shaft through the village... alone. Don Camillo's nemesis was the communist mayor of the village and they had recently again crossed swords. Hence, Tony surmised, was the reason the good padre was carrying the crucifix and shaft alone. Tony vaguely remembers that Don Camillio had a conversation with God. During this one man procession, the Don asked Christ on the cross a question regarding the virtues of socialism and the erring ways of communism... and Christ merely reminds Don Camillo that "he is not a politician but a carpenter."

For some strange reason, Tony has embraced the wisdom in that response and... through many various situations... positions... trying moments... has found comfort in... *I am not a politician, I am a carpenter...* The simplicity of it still captures his spirit.

It has been years and years now that the priest and altar boys/altar servers no longer come out for mass via an adjoining vestibule, but rather from the rear of the church. The newer churches have built the vestibule in the rear. The little procession now comes right down the center aisle of the church and the priest no longer carries his chalice. He follows an altar boy who is carrying a shaft with a crucifix fixed upon the top of it, then the other servers, a boy and a girl and then a 'reader' carrying a large, normally red book, only inches from his face. The parishioners all stand.

Tony also stands at the beginning of the Holy Mass, but always turns his head and watches the small procession walk slowly by him down the aisle. He has over the years developed this little self ritual, whereby when the raised crucifix passes he gently traces a small cross on his forehead with the nail of his thumb, and does the same over his lips and once more over his heart. *In my mind and on my lips and in my heart… what do I know about how to live and how to die… I am only a carpenter…*

Tony wondered… *when did dat start??? dat carrying the cross???* The Romans with their SPQR standards… a private in the Civil War picking up a fallen flag and earning his *red badge of courage… that skinny little altar boy???…so serious so solemn.*

Pg Up

The story telling continued around that happy table. Eyebrows would raise and fall and "tsks" were audible, expressing a sorrow or a pity. And laughter would burst forth and echo off of the ceiling and back down to the linoleum covered floor. Many… if not all of those in attendance would remember that Sunday afternoon dinner for days and months to come. Father and son were telling of their days in the West Virginia coal mines. They had lived it and told it with lips of those who had seen it with their own eyes.

At the start and for only pennies a day, young Pepe was given the responsibility of leading a donkey in and out of the dark mine in the side of a mountain. The donkey would pull a coal cart on a narrow gauge rail line deep into the bowels of the earth. At the end of the rail line was a staging area where some miners would fill the cart with chunks of coal. Pepe would unhitch the donkey and lead him to the other end of the cart and hitch him back to his burden again, this time facing the way they came in. When the cart was full, Pepe would gently tug the lead cord and cluck. The old donkey would first lean a bit in sort of a tug at the breast strap testing the weight of the full cart. Then he'd drop his haunches a few inches and digging down his rear legs start to pull the cart. Inertia was overcome.

When beast, boy and the full coal car reached a slight curve in the rail line and still in the darkness of the mine, the young boy would throw an old blanket over the donkey's head. He'd give it a little shake, protesting the new… newer… darkness but would nonetheless keep his pace forward.

Beyond that slight curve… maybe two hundred feet… was the mine entrance and still another staging area to dump the coal.

Both Pepe and his father explained the covering of the donkey's head and eyes was to prevent him from eventually going blind. A blind mule was not as valuable as a sighted mule. The crew boss told Pepe the first day on the job… he… he with an immortal soul and the God given gift of sight… could be replaced much more easily than a four legged animal. Eventually, Pepe joined his father in the mines with the other miners. The company owned the picks and shovel, and the donkeys, and to a certain extent… the miners.

The story of the donkey fascinated the audience. In their dialect a donkey is called a "ChooCha"… and when used to describe a person, it is not complimentary. Young Michael thought that is why they call them choo-cha and then he asked himself *who is them??*… He wasn't sure… the miners or the donkey. Carmella felt sorry for the donkey and wondered if the animal was ever happy… if he ever frolicked. She knew that the animal could never be as happy as she was at this date… because she was going home… HOME!!! …even now she would frighten herself into thinking something would change it… *Please God, No… no… No…* she reassured herself… *Joseph told me…* and she saw his wife give Govanni an envelope with tickets in it.

Zia Grazia wondered… other than the reality and a certain small amount of inconvenience, *how much more valuable is a donkey that could see as compared to one that can not… So long as the animal could continue pulling the cart… why she'd make a point of getting a sound but blind donkey if they were cheaper.* Uncle Joe thought, the miners… the men… the men themselves were treated with as much dignity as an animal… or a pick and shovel. "Hump!!!" he said almost aloud, "what can you expect for a race of people that teach us to blow our noses into a piece of cloth and then carry it around in our back pocket and call it progress and civil."

And Enzo, who is now sporting a fine full mustache on his upper lip to look older and more mature and manly... thought and compared the donkey's existence with his own... *I work for what seems like nothing... and I work hard... like the choo-cha... what future do either of us have??? One to go blind and the other to only work and never live??*

Pg Dn

Sipping some wine in the back porch, Tony recalled a hot day in June of 1976. He was very certain of the year. There was a hullabaloo about the bicentennial coming on the Fourth of July. Business took him to Philadelphia that day, and it just happened to coincide with a covered wagon caravan that traveled from either Oregon or California, and had arrived that day in downtown Philly. Tony's appointment was also downtown, by the Public Ledger Building and Independence Hall.

Traffic was a little bit more congested than usual, *but what the heck did you expect in the middle of summer and a bicentennial celebration a few weeks away.* However, he managed to park in a nearby subterranean parking lot, and took the steps up to the street. Those underground parking elevators are not always the most hygienically clean or aromatic. When he got topside, he walked smack into the covered wagons coming down Sixth Street. It was a sight... and Tony thought... *I'm gunna tell the kids about this... I'll bet it'll be on the eleven o'clock news.*

Looking back however, what Tony remembers as much as the sight of that stream of covered wagons on Philadelphia streets was the stench of several droppings upon the pavements of the City of Brotherly Love. He once told a friend about this incident and his friend, an authority on vehicles and the history of the internal combustion engine, told him that the gasoline engine was welcomed back at the turn of the century because of that very reason, the stench of horse manure.

And Tony finished that glass of wine, looked into the bottom of the bottle through its green neck and mused *the smell of horse shit or the smell of smog... if the ont don't git you... the other one will.*

When he was finally in bed that particular night a long forgotten memory returned. He was just a kid and in those days the milk man made deliveries from a milk wagon. The milk man had already made his delivery to the La Tarza's house, up and down, mother and daughter, and was making his deliveries at the Salerno house. While the milk man ran to the alleyway and into the house via the rear entrance, his horse relieved himself. The deposit steamed on the pavement of Catherine Street. Later, old man, Mister Bolletieri, came out with an empty bushel basket and a shovel. He filled the bushel basket and returned to his home and went to his back yard. He placed his newly found treasure around his tomato plants. It would eventually work into the soil.

Yeah... Tony thought just before dropping off to sleep... stench is better than smog... smog screws up your respiratory system... but stench... like a hangover, goes away. Yeah, so much for progress and change for the better. He was asleep before too long.

The Insurance Policy

Pg Up

It was a Sunday afternoon and Uncle Joe had just gotten up from his nap. He went into the kitchen, no one was there; then he noticed the door to the bathroom was open and saw his frail Carmella stooping over the bathtub rim, poking down 'air pockets' that were forming from the soaking sheets and pillow cases. The air pockets trapped the steam of the hot water and lifted small portions of the sheets above the waterline. They looked like the top half of white balloons floating in the bathtub water. She was poking at them to make sure they deflated and got that 'good soaking'. Uncle Joe smelled the bleach and then asked if he could use the bathroom. Little Carmella almost knocked herself out hurrying to get out of his way and apologized profusely for being in the way.

Uncle Joe just smiled warmly and said, "E niente." (It is nothing) "I'll be done soon." In passing, she smiled at him and said, "It is good that you are now up, I can go ahead and change the sheets on your bed." She scurried directly to his master bed room.

Uncle Joe urinated, buttoned up his fly and went back into the kitchen while lifting his suspenders over his shoulders. He went to the nearby cupboard, got a Tuscan cigar from a box of five and sat at the kitchen table. He was lighting up the cigar as Carmella re-entered the room on her way to the bathroom with her arms full of sheets and pillowcases. She always showed that sense of urgency… to please… to do what is right… and… never, never make anyone angry.

"Where is everybody?" he asked his sister. He knew where they were, but he wanted her to slow down a bit, relax, maybe even coax her to sit down voluntarily. But, she only ventured as far as the bathroom door and looking over her shoulder at the bathtub and bubbling sheets she told him that they all went to the amusement park. So much for coaxing, Uncle Joe gave up, and theatrically extended his arm toward her, his hand wide opened and palm upward, motioned her to the nearest empty chair at the table and then said in a soft and inviting tone, "a sette per la mour di Dio (sit for the love of God.!)." She did obey, but only after another quick peek at the soaking sheets, and quietly sat at the designated chair. She looked down and away from her brother's eyes.

"Would you like a glass of milk?" shuddering, she said no. "How are you feeling?? …are you taking the medicine Doctor Rossi gave you??" With an extended and exaggerated bobbing of her head, she replied yes. "Didn't you want to go to the park?"…no answer from her… "Didn't you??", Uncle Joe asked again. With a shrug of her shoulder she conveyed no, or maybe even… no, it is nothing for me. Her older brother pressed on, "perche??" (Why??)

She found her voice and softly said, as if in a confessional box, "There is a lot of noise and confusion and pushing and shoving… I don't like it. Besides, I've got things to do here," and she remembered the sheets soaking in the tub and turned her head to see them. She half got out of her chair.

"A sette!!!" (Sit!!), Uncle Joe ordered. His tone was more serious, but not harsh. He smiled at her and puffed on his cigar. For an instant, she looked directly into his eyes and noticed the smile through the bluish gray smoke of the cigar and knew she had not angered him. She looked away shyly.

In the peaceful silence, Uncle Joe studied her and wondered about her future. *She doesn't go to the amusement park because maybe nobody ever asked her.* His wife… as efficient and frugal and religious as she is… doesn't even consider her a second class member of the family… *why should she?? …she doesn't bring a busta (pay envelope) home!!* He felt a shame and a sadness that made him uncomfortable; he wanted to lighten her worries.

"Did you know that your sister Maria Nicola wrote this week??" Still looking away, she smiled and shook her head no. "Grazia is going to marry Donato in June and Chiara is helping the nuns at the Church of the Accession… and… and…" he droned on bringing her up to date. He wondered why nobody told her about the letter… *just second class… not important like most of us… what has this little frail thing done to deserve this fate???…What??*

At a pitch even lower than her normal whisper, she asked, "Guiseppe," she never addressed him by their family's nickname, always Joseph, "Can I go?" twisting her neck and head toward the bathroom door. "I have got to go back and finish."

Uncle Joe smiled warmly, looked at the end of his nose, wagged his head yes, and resigned himself to the fact that his sister just could not relax or loosen up and said aloud, "Va, va, va!!!" (Go, go, go!!!) "But, take it easy." (Va piano). He finished his cigar, got up from the kitchen chair, buttoned his vest, put on his suit coat and got his hat. As he opened the kitchen door to the staircase, he turned slightly and told her, "I am going to Goomba Tomasino's." At the head of the staircase he turned back once again and added, "*Stata a tenda!*" *(Stay alert… be careful!).*

The usual Sunday afternoon crowd was at Tomasino's. It was a Sunday crowd because, at this time of the year, a few of the construction workers that came in last night with Enzo and Michael from New Berlin were there. Uncle Joe first stood at the bar but after the glass of wine, felt the bar railing was much too crowded for his taste. He ordered another wine, looked around and spotted an empty table. He motioned Tomasino that he was going to it. Tomasino called out to him, "Good, I want to see you for a minute." Uncle Joe nodded his acknowledgment and made his way to the empty table.

He noticed Alberino at the far end of the long, beautiful mahogany bar getting "wasted." He sipped his wine and smacked his lips a little… *this wine is not bad…* he thought to himself and just then he happened to notice Tomasino and his brother-in-laws Pasqual and Nicolo, who ran a grocery store, all putting their heads together and occasionally looking back at him. *I wonder what the hell they are talking about*, he said to himself and quickly added, *well, if it concerns me they'll tell me...* and he took another sip of wine. He was about to find out.

Tomasino poured two glasses of wine, called his cousin from the kitchen to watch the bar for him, and with the two glasses stepped around the back of the bar to the table area. He made his way to Uncle Joe's table. He was followed by both Pasqual and Nicolo, carrying their beer glasses. Tomasino put one of the wine glasses in front of Uncle Joe and sat down. The other two joined the party. Cautiously, Uncle Joe looked at all three of them, squinted and said aloud, "What the hell? Is this gunna cost me money or what?? Whaddaya you guys want?"

The new arrivals laughed at his questions. "So how are you today my fine friend?" Tomasino wanted to know. Uncle Joe did not answer, but looked at all three of them without moving his head... only his eyes. Pasqual sensing the uncomfortable feeling of the pregnant pause, and the effect of the new arrivals to Joe's table, took a stab at injecting some humor and bravely said, "Hey Joe, I saw Johnny the Midget (the door man at the local brothel) and he said he hasn't seen you lately... You find yourself a little *commara* or something?? The Africanos miss you, he told me." They all laughed except Uncle Joe.

Uncle Joe ended that effort to lighten the atmosphere with an icing and menacing stare. Wanting to steer the conversation to a more amicable tone, Tomasino quickly cleared his throat and asked Joe "how everything was going and inquired about the health of his charges." Uncle Joe gave him a slight nod and responded "everybody was okay".

Tomasino continued, "You know Doctor Rossi stopped in here for a glass of wine last week and we got to talking. Tony, the shoemaker's kid, is pretty sick with pneumonia but he thinks the kid is over the worse of it. He also told me he stopped by to see your sister, Carmella; she is such a petite thing. How is she doing?"

"She is getting better."

"Good!!! Good!!!" Tomasino said and then repeated himself, "Good!! Good!!...we are glad to hear it." *We???* *We??? Who's including these two guys???... they wouldn't know Carmella if she came in here and sat on my lap."* After another slight pause Tomasino continued.

"Good" he said and repeated himself, "Good! Good, glad to hear it!" After another momentary pause, he added, "she is so small and frail we all tend to worry about her."

Still another pregnant pause... uncomfortable... and the two uninvited guests got the fidgets. Tomasino, the leader, again went into the breech... he had to... he had a plan... and if it was to materialize, it would have to be done soon... now!

"Pepe" he opened to Uncle Joe again, using the informal friendly nickname for Joseph "Aey, there are a lotta expenses and worry keeping the family under control and everything else... every thing costs so much these days." His brother-in-law and the grocer nodded sympathetically and with solemn eyes looked back at Uncle Joe. Uncle Joe nodded in turn and kept thinking... *Where is he going with this???*

With the ground work laid out and reinforced by Uncle Joe's nod, "You know, Pepe, as much as we all love her, (...*there he goes with that 'WE' again*) that little sweet Carmella is not long for this world and I'm sure there is a special place for her in Heaven... with all the Angels." They all nodded yes, with sad and down turned eyes.

Uncle Joe just said "Spariamo." (Let's hope.)

... and now for his move... Tomasino continued, "After Doctor Rossi left last week, Frank Vernido... the insurance man stopped by and we got to talking. He, like all of us here... realized that there would be an additional expense for a funeral to you and Commarra Grazia, at this (he quickly changed the word to), at that time." Uncle Joe was no longer moving his eyes from the grocer to his brother-in-law, but fixed them directly into Tomasino's face and eyes. (...*ah ...he thought and almost said aloud... a quasi va u fatto* (so this is where he is going) ...*he wants me to buy a life policy from Frank... but why are these other guys here?? ...he should have Frank here.*)

He interrupted Tomasino and said... "Let us think about the girl's good health and I can manage my household."

"Oh... I am sure you can... we all know that... for sure!!! But, an opportunity presented itself which will benefit everybody at this table." Uncle Joe raised his chin signaling to Tomasino he was curious and was coaxing him on.

"We all got expenses... future expenses... Pasqual has three daughters to marry off, Nicolo has a twenty year mortgage... me... you know some of my problems... I always need a dollar I don't have..." they all nodded in unison, except Uncle Joe.

"NOW!!! Now is the moment!!"

"Frank the insurance man said that for twenty five dollars a year... for ten years... we could buy a four thousand dollar life policy on Carmella. She is comparatively young and that is why it is so reasonable... we... me and Pasqual and Nicolo, are willing to pay the premium, and when the time comes... God forbid... we will get a thousand apiece and the other is for you and Commarra Grazia... no expense to you!!! ...my wife was talking to Grazia the other day and she liked the idea... (Uncle Joe thought... *I bet she would*)... but we need you Pepe... because you are her legal guardian and she is in your household... you have got to sign the application." Tomasino paused, took a breath and concluded, "Whaddya say, Pepe?"

Lots of thoughts flashed across Uncle Joe's mind... his sister... their conversation that afternoon... the smell of bleach... the bubbles of soaking bed sheets... Carmella's sad eyes… never asking… but just conveying hope… *when does she smile???… Does she ever, just smile?… I don't know… but she is not happy here… America is not for everybody… she was happy up until she came to Ellis Island and was still with Pa… she should have returned with him… eh ?… who knew that then! …these guys say 'we' have an opportunity… it is a matter of timing… those sad eyes across the table… that little creature fidgeting in her chair… a matter of timing… it could be an opportunity for her!!!*

Why not?? She deserves a little bit more of life… it is an opportunity to send her back home and give her just a bit more happiness these last few years of her life…

I'll make my mark on this lousy piece of paper… and send her back… Tomasino, Pasqual, Nicolo, Frank and my wife will all be happy… and… finally… so will Carmella!!! …let my wife and her sisters clean the dishes and poke down the soaking sheets… and smell the bleach.

Uncle Joe told them, "Okay." The visitors to his table all smiled broadly and Nicolo pulled out papers from his coat jacket; Tomasino quickly went back behind the bar and returned to the table with a small inkwell and a pen. They

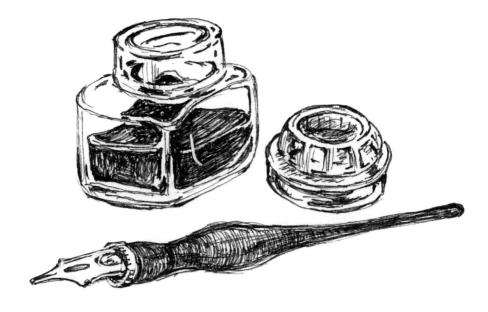

cleaned the table space in front of Uncle Joe; he dipped the neb of the pen into the ink well and then he placed his name on the application. And he thought again, *it is a matter of timing and an opportunity for everyone, especially for Carmella.*

Uncle Joe remained at Tomasino's bar for the remainder of the evening and became very, very inebriated. Tomasino had to send for his kid brothers, Enzo and Michael, to help Uncle Joe home. Each of the brothers grabbed an arm and then draped it over their shoulders. As Uncle Joe staggered to his feet, he mumbled… "America is not for everybody."

The boys looked at one another; half giggled and shrugged their shoulders.

Young Michael, always the bold one, ventured forth and asked, "What do you mean, Joseph?'

Uncle Joe did not immediately reply, but only looked across the bar room and saw Alberino half nodding, half sleeping, still on his feet, standing at the bar railing. He thought of Alberino and Alberino's wife. He only repeated, "America is not for everyone." The boys giggled at what they only thought to be a drunken man's words.

The boys dutifully took him home and to put him into his bed under the watchful eye of Zia Grazia. She had a look of disdain and angrily reminded her husband that he was to start work in less than five hours. The boys undressed him and put him to bed.

Uncle Joe smelled the clean freshness of the sheets and for a reason he himself did not understand, smiled to himself and drifted off into a total slumber.

Early Morning Flight

Mr. Aldo Sabitano came from the mountains out-side of Foggia and was a well respected man throughout the Italian community of Utica. The story was... he was well educated by the local priest and nuns, way up in the mountains, and all who knew him were certain he would become a priest... and because he was so smart... a bishop.

His mother especially, dreamed of the day... in her old age... and after she was widowed... of becoming the cook in the rectory of her son's parish. Her wonderful visions of the future were of a full pantry (for priests seldom, if ever, went hungry in Italy and a table covered with her excellent and always so tasteful food... her pasta and her salads and her special omelets... and her beaten fava beans... so smooth and creamy... it could almost be spread like a delicate cheese... and many... no all!!! ...of the village's most prominent *signori* sitting at the table at one time or another. And her intelligent and handsome son holding court and discussing solutions to all the ills of mankind and... all... each and every one... enjoying her cooking). What wonderful and happy dreams she had... but it was not her destiny... for her Aldo came to la'Merica early in 1911 shortly before the Italo-Turkish War... he married and had two sons and one daughter.

Mr. Sabitano worked hard and he and his petite wife, from outside of Bari, skimped and saved and they purchased a small home on Clay Street. Mr. Sabitano quickly taught himself to read and write English and soon became Mr. Perretta's right hand man at the bank. Mr. Perretta recognized very early Aldo's value and paid him very well. To him, it was a long term investment to, one, keep Aldo in his employ and, two, happy. Should Aldo have ever decided to strike out on his own, Mr. Perretta knew that he would really have very serious competition. Should he, Mr. Perretta, have such apprehensions and fears, they were unfounded, because Mr. Aldo Sabitano had no lofty ambitions. He was a devoted family man and their well being and happiness and education was his only driving force.

Why... his eldest son, Louis, was doing very, very well in school, so much so that Mrs. Warlock... a very wealthy but childless widow of a coal baron... had taken him under her protective wing... loaning him and other talented and bright immigrant children, Poles... Russians... Syrians... Lebanese... books and having them over as guests to her home. They would have a mild tea or lemonade in her front parlor on Sunday afternoons. They would read poetry and discuss the classics. In time, Mrs. Warlock would direct and steer all these select children to Columbia University or Hamilton College or Colgate or Syracuse, at times even offering a small financial grant. Yes, Mrs. Warlock had grand visions for the small elite group of immigrant children... and she... SHE... the renowned Mrs. Warlock... picked Mr. Aldo Sabitano's eldest son for this group. They... even at this early age... were so proud of their son, Louis, a humble and respectful boy.

Every work day Aldo Sabitano, immaculately dressed, in a white shirt with a detachable collar and tie, and a neatly buttoned vest that matched his suit, and a black derby 'dress-up' hat, would leave his little one and a half story home with a refinished attic dormer for the boys' bedroom, with a brown paper bag containing his lunch. He would walk the half block south on Clay to Catherine St., turn left and walk past Brandegee School. There was talk that the school was already too small to accommodate the children and plans were being discussed for expanding... more than doubling the class rooms. In years to come, it would happen and the kids going to the school would refer to the different sections as 'the old building and the new building' even though it was still one school.

Mr. Sabitano could easily have crossed through the Brandegee School yard to get onto Jay Street, a short cut to his work, but did not. He felt, maybe believed is a better word to use, that the school and the school yard belonged to the children and to the school, and he felt that by walking thereon for one's own selfish reason was wrong and a small violation of ethics. That's how much he respected education and its quasi-holy halls.

At the corner of Kossuth and Catherine Streets he would turn right and continue up Kossuth right past Tony Marraffa's Fish & Poultry Market. About a year ago, Tony had some sort of trouble and his wife came to Mr. Perretta's bank for a modest ninety day loan to pay for some unforeseen medical bills and a short hospital stay for Tony. Aldo, because he saw the value of the man and the work ethic of him and his wife, recommended approval of the loan, and although Mr. Perretta was a little hesitant (he was leery because of the rumored cause of Mr. Marraffa's hospital stay and facial surgery), nonetheless accepted Aldo's recommendation, and the loan was approved.

The loan was repaid in a prompt and timely manner. On this particular day, as Mr. Sabitano walked by, Tony Marraffa was outside at the street curb inspecting and verifying his weekly delivery of fish from Boston. The truck driver and his assistant were unloading the crates of fish from the rear of the large two and half ton truck, putting the crates on a two wheeled upright cart, pausing momentarily in front of Tony for his quick count and then scurrying into the fish store and quickly returning for another load. Tony's two large shiny black Belgian Police dogs would quietly follow the delivery men in and out of the fish store and then return to Tony's heel. Tony, standing on the sidewalk wearing his white full length apron and boots, touched the visor of his cap when he saw Mr. Sabitano and said "Buon Giorno Don Aldo!!"

Mr. Sabitano smiled genuinely and nodded acceptance of the greeting, the dogs wagged their tails and made room for Aldo to pass. Tony Marraffa made it a point always to touch the brim of his hat whenever he greeted Don Aldo. He seldom if ever, extended that little hand gesture courtesy to other men, especially Mr. Perretta and Don Salvatore. Continuing his uninterrupted walk to work, which is now within sight, the southwest corner of Jay Street and Kossuth Avenue, Mr. Sabitano thought how nicely that scar on Tony Marraffa's face was healing. It had lost its pinkness and a day or two of not shaving almost made it unnoticeable. He continued the thought by adding... *maybe he should grow a nicely cropped beard, like General Garibaldi.*

He arrived at the bank and dutifully unlocked the front door, raised the shades over the three large glass plates, went around the caged counter, placed his lunch in the bottom left hand drawer of his desk, took off his suit coat and arranged it on a wooden clothes hanger, shook it a bit... as if to cleanse it from non-existent dust... and placed it on the clothes tree a few feet behind his desk. When he sat at his desk, he methodically opened the bottom right hand drawer and retrieved two neatly folded black tubular half sleeves from the drawer, snapped each in turn and pulled them over his arms up to his elbows.

He was pondering whether or not to use the green shade visor and was studying the outside lighting from one of the big plate glass windows to his front. The front door opened and two young women entered, they were Miss

Angelina Salerno and Mrs. Pauline Jones. Pauline, whose maiden name was Carfola and was recently married. It was exactly 8:25, and the Perretta Bank would be opened for business at eight thirty.

Mr. Perretta would always arrive... just on *the inside* of the hour or *the outside* of the hour... and the hour being 9:00 a.m. Today it was 9:03, according to his own gold pocket watch, which had three different types of gold in the chain. The employees soberly greeted him, and he nodded his recognition and walked to his office in the rear. As was Pauline's custom or routine, she'd scurry quickly back into the small lunch room with a tabletop single-ringed cooking jet, take the warm coffee pot filled with six cups of hot espresso, place it on a wooden tray with two demitasse cups and saucers, a small round sugar bowl with a spoon's nose burned into the center, two miniature spoons and two cloth napkins. She then carried the tray into Mr. Perretta's office. She met Mr. Sabitano by the door, and smiled broadly with a little curtsy, nod at him, where upon he quietly said thank you to her. Mr. Sabitano... the one the villagers dreamed of becoming a Bishop... entered the three sided glass office and closed the door behind him. Mr. Perretta loved his black coffee sweet and not only did he put three spoons of sugar into his little demitasse cup... only half filled... he capped it off... up to the brim with anisette. The bottle was kept in the lower left hand drawer of his massive desk, and before he replaced the cap, he extended his arm a bit, pointed the neck of the bottle to Aldo and with a slight jerk of his head and a half bounce of his wrist inquired if he would part take.

Aldo shot both hands up to shoulder level, made a pushing gesture, smiled warmly and said, "Te reingrazia tanto, ma non!" (I thank you very much, but no). Mr. Perretta replaced the cork and returned the bottle to his desk drawer and closed the drawer.

And now to the business at hand… and today's business was Alberino the baker. Mr. Perretta shook his head sadly and frowned, interlaced his fingers and seemed to study them. He looked from under his eyebrows at Aldo and finally said aloud, "Your instincts were correct when you objected to renting the bakery to him… but looking back it seemed that he might be able to make it work… he worked for Nicotera's bakery over on the other side of Mohawk Street, got married to that younger girl… the bakery had been vacant for months after Pasqual Coliccio went back to Pescara… and we had to prove our worth in being named as absentee *padronos* (landlords)… the people were getting used to not having a bakery on that location and going to other neighborhoods to buy their bread…. I don't know… it just seemed like it might work out." He unclasped his hands and fingers, leaned back in his chair, took another swig of coffee, paused another moment and then looked Aldo straight in his eyes and asked, "Why were you so sure it was doomed to fail???"

"Oh I don't really know," Aldo paused for a second or two and then continued, "but I had this feeling and I didn't really approve of how he treated his first wife… the way he acted during her sickness… the way he treats his new wife in public… and she, herself, is just a young, confused, frightened, little girl… who tries very hard to do the right thing… she could easily have become a loving wife and a good mother to any other man who had a strand of decency in him… but I guess the most obvious reason was I felt he was a selfish, self-centered man, just the kind of man who should never drink… never drink…" Aldo repeated it, "never drink" and concluded by saying, "such men make very bad business partners."

Mr. Peretta nodded in agreement and said, "Yes… Yes… I should have grasped that when you told me. Griffin, the flour man, will no longer extend him any credit whatsoever, even when he has a glut of inventory... I should have seen it coming."

A plan was made; Alberino would be given an opportunity to save face... so to say... his bankers as emissaries of the owner in Pescara, would offer him the chance to turn over the management of his little bakery... to a more experienced baker-business man... like Luigi Rintrona or Giuseppe and wife... all very successful... good money handlers. He will not have to manage any money whatsoever, he would receive a reasonable pay and 'free' boarding of the apartment over the bakery.

The alternative was he would have to file bankruptcy and be put out onto the street. He was currently four months in arrears of his rent already and having troubles with his supplier. Mr. Sabitano and Mr. Perretta could no longer dun him for payments. The offer was fair under the circumstances. It was decided that both Mr. Perretta and Mr. Sabitano would go and visit him that very afternoon.

They did so at 1:30 that day. Alberino resisted but eventually agreed... his wife just stood quietly near the bedroom door curtain. After the men with fine suits, ties and derby hats left, Anna Maria wept silently into her handkerchief. She was very frightened for her, their, future very frightened.

That next morning before dawn, Alberino and his wife bundled their skimpy and limited wardrobe and snuck out into the night, abandoning all.

Flight to Boston.... Ashes Ashes

Anna Maria had a rough time keeping up with Alberino as they headed down Bleecker Street to Third Avenue, turned north for two short blocks and came upon the farmers' market. Alberino's sense of urgency was strange to his wife; it seemed to curb the meanness he always showed to her. It seemed to her he had a strangeness in his eyes, something she had not seen before… a sort of panicky, wide eyed fear… and his eyes were blood-shot. She realized after a few blocks down the darkened streets, that they… she, herself… were fleeing from something. For some strange reason, after that realization, her bundle of clothing seemed to get heavier.

Various sized trucks and an occasional horse drawn wagon, were already there and the market was open and conducting business. Five streets converged at that spot and formed a circle. The farm vehicles (motorized and not), were parked on the semi-grassy circular mall, with their front tires resting on the grass, having jumped the curb and crossed the sidewalk that ringed the grassy mall. By the end of the growing season, the truck tires and the wagon wheels beat the struggling grass into submission. The farmers would partially unload the produce from their vehicles on, under, and by the tailgates of their vehicles and barter with customers. The customers were owners of grocery stores or vegetable stores and an occasional owner, or two, of a push cart.

There was the hustle and bustle… mostly men… of early morning activity at a working, prosperous, city open market. The entire scene was illuminated by the city street-lights, which were soon to pale in the morning light.

Alberino spotted a large green truck with a silver colored fish in the center and on both side wall panels of the body of the truck. Above and below the fish was lettering that proudly told everyone in the world that the truck belonged to the Boston Fish Market, 1717 Prince Street, Boston, Mass.

Alberino, like so many of the peasant immigrant mountain people of Italy, did not know how to read, but he recognized the truck, having often seen it at Tony Marraffa's fish market. He knew people who came to America and entered through Boston and Providence, Rhode Island. Boston was a large city like Neuva Yorka, and he and his wife could find some work there... there was always work for women in the textile mills, even here in Utica. But, he admitted to himself that he owed too many people too much money here in Utica, furthermore textile mills were for women, unless you were a 'cutter' who got a nickel more an hour. But, Alberino felt that, too, was beneath him.

Anna Maria could find some kind of work there and in time he could find work in his field.

His wife was a pace or two behind him as they circled the big green truck. When they got back to the left rear wheel of the truck, Alberino tossed his smaller bundle against the tire, took a half step away and like a master signaling his dog, he shot out his arm and pointed his index finger at his bundle, indicating to Anna Maria to put her bundle there too. He said, "Stay here!!" and started to walk away.

Disoriented in a new surrounding, not knowing what was happening... so confused, Anna Maria ventured to inquire and in a very low quiet voice asked Alberino, "A dau va?? E perche a questa ora?? Nona ja enpasta la farina??" (Where are we going?? And why at this hour... don't you have to mix the flour for bread??)

His nerves... this running away made him very impatient and kind of frightened and excitable. He stopped suddenly; half turned, raised his right arm across his chest ready to backhand this nagging woman and hissed... "Stata zita!!! Sta qua!!!" (Be quiet/shut up... Stay here!!) He did not strike out at her this time, but he came close to beating her again. He stormed off to an all night 'cantenna' where some of the farmers, truck drivers and store owners congregated to have some wine, negotiate sales, and smoke Tuscany cigars. John 'the Midget' Pape, the always recognizable door man from the cat house on Third Avenue, would come around about four a.m., buy a few select cantina customers a glass of wine or two and entice them over to Don Salvatore's brothel. (Three lousy bucks for the time of your life… and something you won't forget until you get that commara again… white or colored!!!)

Farmers with profit from their crop, grocery store owners and fruit and vegetable store owners with money saved from their bartering talents (or money not spent because the produce they wanted was either too high or not available) and drivers a long way from home and nobody knew their marital status or parents, all made very good prospects for Johnny the Midget.

Eddie O'Brien and his younger brother, Sean, were from Boston and their father owned The Boston Fish Market on Prince Street in Boston. They made weekly deliveries… two or three day trips… down the Mohawk Valley to Syracuse, to Rochester and then Buffalo. Today they are heading home. They made arrangements with the Russo Fruit and Vegetable Wholesalers in Boston to pick up forty-five bushels of green beans from a Frankfort farmer named Argento.

This Argento guy was to meet them at this public market today with the forty-five bushels of green beans; he was a little late. But Big Frank Argento finally made it. They transferred the load and the three of them went to the cantina to get a glass of wine and some beer. (The O'Brien boys… especially the eldest, avoided 'dago red' because he once got looped on it and had nightmares for a solid week… that experience even frightened off his younger brother and he never even tried it.) Big Frank had no such qualms. The Irish boys gave him the check from Mr. Russo and he was happy for the quick sale of almost half his bean crop for that picking. However, as much as he hated to leave their company and the good times in the cantina, he had to go back to the cultivator and those two huge tomato fields... a two day job. He gave enough money to the barkeep for at least another three drinks apiece for the O'Brien boys. Big Frank was generous in his recently acquired wealth.

Eddie, being the oldest and 'more mature', was in charge of the road money for routine expenses. With that Big Guy's donation to the beer kitty, they had a couple of bucks left over (...outside of gasoline expense which they both knew was more than covered...) to either get plastered or get laid. The sons of the owner of the wholesale fish market in Boston decided to buy a full gallon of dago red... to bring to Mr. Russo when they dropped off the forty-five bushels of beans... hoping to exchange the tightly sealed gallon full of 'the good stuff' from a real genuine neighborhood for one of those bushels of fresh green beans.

They were about to pick up their beers and go first to the bar keep for the gallon (and any change) and then go talk to Johnny the Midget, when out of nowhere, Alberino appeared and sat at their table.

In his surprise Eddie just bounced back off of the rear of his café seat. The seat's backrest had two circular loops meeting and looping at the top and then returning to the chair's seat. Sean half leaned and half headed forward, anticipating trouble. Eddie spoke first and said in a threatening tone, "What the fuck do you want???" to the little, nervous man who un-expectably joined them at the table.

Alberino explained he wanted to go to Boston. Sean, the younger and not yet married brother, angrily replied, "Get the fuck out, you creep, or I'll kick your ass into next week sometime." But no... he must get to Boston... he had to get to Boston... we could ride in the back of the truck. Sean didn't want to hear any nonsense and was rising out of his seat, when Eddie, with a raised and opened hand signaled him to sit back down.

"Boston is more than four hundred miles from here, do you have any money to pay for the gas?" Eddie had the business sense; there was room in the truck, even with all those bushels of beans and this could turn out to be a very profitable day for the delivery men. But… No he did not have any money… but it was important for him and his wife to get to Boston… they could find work there and pay the brothers later.

The same business sense that made Eddie ask if he had any money, made him smirk and bat the air in front of him with an open hand showing disgust at the stupid suggestion. Even young Sean knew that if they did throw them in the back of the truck, once they got to Boston he'd disappear as quickly as cigar smoke and never be seen again.

"Get lost… who do you think you are bullshitting??" Eddie was about to tell his brother to get rid of him. Alberino just had to get to Boston… he could not stay in Utica any longer… and then he saw and recognized Johnny the Midget and knew why he was there. He turned quickly to Eddie, who Alberino by now knew was the leader and the more reasonable of the two, stooped over a bit and leaned forward and whispered… that he could give him his wife for ten, fifteen minutes… to… how to say??? satisfy any natural and healthy *wants* he may possess.

Eddie leaned back again and his eyebrows raised, Sean who heard the offer laughed and said to Alberino, "If she is as old and as ugly as you… who the hell would want her??" But no!! No!! She was much younger and plump in the right places… seventeen years younger than him… pretty face… you both could have your carnal craving pleasantly sedated… ten minutes twenty minutes… as much time as you need… both of you!! Yes!!! Yes!!!… both of you. The older brother just shook his head… not believing what he was hearing, the younger looking at Alberino in amazement, which then changed to excitement. He darted a quick look at his older brother... his expression conveyed his thoughts... *What the hell? We were just going to go over to the cat house and spend good money... on the very same thing this asshole is offering.*

Eddie looked into his younger sibling's face and read his thoughts as easily as if they were said aloud. He then turned to Alberino and asked, "Where is she??" He replied, "By the green truck." With a jerk of his head, Ed dispatched his brother and said..."See what she looks like and see if it is worth it." Sean eagerly nodded and quickly went out.

Sean found her right where Alberino left her: two bundles by her feet and propped against the rear tire of the truck... the one with the large silver fish painted on its side. Their eyes met and it quickly registered with him she was indeed young... much younger than the old man. His eyes dropped down to her bust line, and even though she had a loose inexpensive dress on, he could see she was plump in the right spots and petite, as well as shapely. He had had worse... and this one wasn't bad at all!!

Anna Maria looked at this man staring at her in the middle of the night... by the back of a truck... with strange men working around, and she was very frightened. It was obvious to Sean that the girl was petrified by his gawking, his eyes were wide, and his nostrils flared a bit, he felt the surge of desire throughout his body. He shook his head in an attempt to come back to and it worked. Boy!! He was ready to run back to the cantina and get Eddie... right away!! But she had better be there when he came back, so he thought he would lock her there, by the rear wheel of a big truck with a large silver fish painted on its side, and said to her sternly, "You ain't stealing any of those beans in the back of the truck, are you???"

He spoke much too fast in that New England accent for Anna Maria to understand even one word of the question, this was not Scully Square in Boston with drunken sailors walking about. She didn't understand a single word, but the tone of his voice, the look on his face, made her instinctively shake her head no. She watched him with a fear that made her revisit and relive that beating her father gave her years ago.

Sean sensed the power he had over this frightened, petite but 'plump breasted' woman and added in an even more menacing tone, "You stay right here" and he pointed to the ground and the bundles by the truck, "I'm going to get your husband and we'll be right back!!!" Anna Maria understood most of that... hand gesture down to the ground... "stay here"... the English word for marrito... 'husband'... and surmised, correctly, that he was going to get Alberino. She was momentarily relieved, but the euphoric feeling would disappear soon enough.

Eddie O'Brien and his brother and the small but mean Alberino all returned to the truck, the largest one of them, Eddie, was carrying a gallon of wine. They stopped by the bundles and Anna Maria. They talked for a minute; all of them smiling and occasionally looking at that petite but... plump breasted... girl, and smiling even more broadly.

Eventually, Eddie went up to the cab of the truck and put the gallon of wine behind the bench seat of the truck and returned. Sean and Alberino threw the bundles into the rear of the truck's enclosed bed. Sean jumped up and arranged the bundles near the rear of the truck bed and then went to the front of the truck bed and rearranged a few of the bushel baskets of beans.

Then Sean came to the rear of truck again and standing on the edge, by the down tailgate, he offered his hand to Anna Maria. She blushed somewhat and reached up and accepted the offered hand and was lifted up into the truck. Eddie and Alberino sort of helped. When Anna Maria was firmly standing in the truck, she expected the young Irishmen to let go of her hand, but he didn't. She was confused and did not understand. She darted a quick, frightened look at Alberino, who merely responded by placing his index finger over his lips… telling her to remain silent and then hissed, "Zita!!! Si non te matsa!!" (Quiet!! Or I'll kill you!!)

Eddie lowered the tarp that acted as three quarters of the back cover of the large green truck with a silver fish painted on the side panels. When the tailgate was up, the tarp could be secured to it. After a while, Sean re-appeared at the tailgate and gingerly jumped out… he was happily smiling. Eddie then reached up, grasped the rim of the tailgate and climbed in, he stooped a bit as he raised the tarp halfway, and then released it and the tarp returned to its full extent and swung for just a moment.

In a while, Eddie too came out of the truck with a slight smile and a contented look. They both arranged the tarp so that the inside of the truck body had some light… half way down the opening above the tail gate… secured the tarp ends to eyelets on the truck side panels, got in the cab and they all drove off to Boston.

Anna Maria eventually came out from behind a wall of bushel baskets… stacked three high and sat on the clothing bundles she had carried that morning. She was across from Alberino, who was sitting on his bundle with his arm draped over the rim of the tailgate, watching Utica fall away from them in the early morning light.

On that long and bumpy ride to Boston, Alberino sneakily opened one of the bushels and ate raw beans. Very uncharacteristically of him, he offered her some raw green beans; she just nodded no and kept gazing out from the back of the truck: the green truck with silver fishes painted on the side panels.

It was the worst day in Anna Maria's life and she seldom ever spoke to Alberino again.

Alma da lasta One-a

Zia Lucia died. The middle of January… Super Bowl week…. January, when the frozen ground does not welcome its dead and a wrapped, motionless fig tree remains chilled and dormant under clear blue skies. She had not been feeling well over the past few days, and coupled with advanced stages of dementia, she appeared to become more cranky and ill tempered, even over the slightest little thing. Her daughters, God love them, would not never… ever… consider a nursing home where twenty-four hour care could be administered. NO!!! Never EVER..!!! These girls, all grown women now… three already widowed, were from the old school. Respect, dignity, honor, obligation and duty were not just meaningless and pretty or empty words to these girls. Seven remaining daughters, one day and night apiece, had stood watch for more than four years. The unexpected interruptions to the routine, which is inevitable, were always handled in an amicable manner; it boiled down to this: *Ma is not to be left alone and certainly not put into the hands of strangers… it's our own blood and flesh for God's sake!*

It happened on Lucy's watch. She had made a bowl of Lipton soup for her mother and try as she may, could not coax her to finish anymore than just half a bowl; and mostly liquid at that. Linda came over on her lunch hour just to see…"How's Ma doing?" Over a cup of coffee (there was always a pot on the stove at Zia Lucia's house), they agreed, *not good*. The dreaded time had arrived, while Linda watched Zia Lucia, Lucy called her sisters and brothers. Like sentinels awaiting orders, the six others girls all arrived within three quarters of an hour. *Where is Sammy and Anthony (DeeBee)? DeeBee is picking up Sammy, Sammy doesn't have his car…*

"Ma… how ya feeling Ma??" Teresa. Same question from Elvira. No response, *she's failing…* Marie Delores… "Ma you wanna lay down?" Zia Lucia rolled her head, eyes half closed… cursed… but did not consent. Carmella, "I'm gunna call an ambulance!!" "Naw… she always wanted this to happen at home with only loved ones around her… we'll help her over the tough spots!!"

Zia Lucia swayed to the right. In a flash, Rita and Carmella left their chairs and were prepared to catch her, but as the gods would have it, Zia Lucia swung violently and quickly to the left and crashed onto her kitchen floor… HER kitchen floor for the past forty six years.

"Oh God!!! Ma!! Ma… ya alright??… Oh my God… Ma, Ma did you get hurt??? Let's get her in bed… I am gunna call an ambulance… help me, help me… somebody grab her other arm." Marie Delores, Rita, Linda and Lucy raised up their fallen mother and started for her bedroom. Elvira and Carmella were leading the way, moving chairs and the end table… Teresa turned down the bed… because they all felt so very hopeless and frightened and wanting to do what was right... some of the girls started to quietly weep… they called for an ambulance.

Within minutes after the collapse, Zia Lucia's two sons arrived with their wives. DeeBee went to pick up Sam because Sam had loaned his car to his son who needed a battery for his jalopy. The brothers looked around and they sensed immediately… *this is it!!*

"We called an ambulance... how's she doing??? Not good… not good at all… Oh God… oh my God…" Rita lamented her failure to catch her falling mother, with tears streaming down her face and staring at the overhead fixture, she was saying aloud, "If I could have only stopped her from hitting the floor… she hit it so hard!!!" "So very, very hard"… and her sobs became even more audible than before.

DeeBee, now the eldest son, went to his weeping sister, gently embraced her and quietly reminded her, "Ma's time has just come… she did not feel the fall or anything else. Her time has just come."

The ambulance arrived; Zia Lucia's two sons and

Lucy went to the hospital. At five minutes past five the phone rang, Marie Delores answered the phone, she noticed the time, 5:05, on the microwave by the kitchen phone. It was Lucy's voice on the other end of the phone: "Marie, ma is gone".... a slight pause... an auditable controlled sob... and then... "We gotta call Donetta and Aunt Clara".... "we already did"... "we gotta call Carmen Ennance too"... "see if he could stop over"..."Yeah... okay... sure... I'll do it right now!!"

Carmen Ennance wanted to date one of the girl's older sisters, Anne Frances. She was called only Frances because her namesake Grandmother never called herself Anna... only Francesca, but Fran wasn't interested in him. She loved and eventually eloped with a Calabrese man from around St. Anthony's church. She 'ran away' to Alabama where her Lucien was. He had recently been activated with his National Guard unit and would eventually go to the Philippines. Carmen had asked several of Francesca's sisters to put in a good word in for him... but Fran was too much in love with her Lucien. Poor Fran was the first to pass away sometime in the early seventies.

Carmen eventually became a successful mortician and through the years still remained close to the nucleus of the Di Risio family. Carmen was the calmest man that Tony (or for that matter anyone in the family) ever knew. Always well dressed, good looking with dark wavy hair, combed straight back and with a soft and pacifying tone of voice. One time Dee Bee and Joey and Tony were discussing Carmen's demeanor... "Do ya tink he ever got excited... or pissed off... or yelled... or didn't smile... or said 'oh shit' or 'fuck it!!'... Do ya??? Naw... never in a zillion years... but... **he had** to get excited a few times... he's got three daughters!" Carmen married a good friend of Donetta, and Donetta was in the bridal party.

"We gotta call Carmen... yeah... okay... sure... I'll do it right now."

By this time all of Zia Lucia's son-in-laws came, bearing gifts: East Utica tomato pie, a large tray of cold cuts from a local super market deli section, and a fruit basket. Two others chipped in and purchased two liters of whiskey (Black Velvet and Four Roses) and a gallon of red table wine and two cases of beer (Utica Club). They did not know what Zia Lucia had in her home (it was substantial), but, they thought… *better safe than sorry.* You see, all of Zia Lucia's son-in-laws were from the old school too. It was dark now and it was getting colder as it always does on clear January nights, that bitter cold that stings your face. The front porch light seemed to have a little halo around it.

A knock on the side porch door… Enter Aunt Clara, followed by Donetta and her husband carrying a big box of cannolis from Carmen's (or was it from the Florentine?) Either one, cannolis were always a treat.

But what ignited… that almost immediately and gratefully transformed a room full of saddened women into half smiles and possibly all thinking… *Ma's gone… but we are all still alive and we gotta live!!*…was cute little Aunt Clara. Taking off her kerchief with two hands, her heavy winter coat appeared to be pushing her down and causing her to sink even more to ground level. She held the flowery flannel kerchief in her right hand, then raised her arms at her side, raised them to shoulder level (her kerchief sort of dangling and waving) and announced to the assembled nieces and nephews and their spouses in a voice tone two octaves above her normal quiet speaking voice… *"**Alma da lasta won-a!!!**"*

Teresa thought of the first time she saw her and of her confirmation day a few years later, and how Aunt Clara never forgot a date or a birthday, or anything. Lucy thought of her birthday, December 12th, which is shared by such famous celebrities as Frank Sinatra and Mayor Ed Koch, (and is also the Feast Day of Our Lady of Guadalupe), but also by her last remaining aunt, Aunt Clara. Twenty years apart… to the day. It was Aunt Clara who first told her the story about the Mexican-Indian peasant who saw Our Lady of Guadalupe and caused great things to happen.

Carmella studied her features and realized that still… after all these years… Aunt Clara's complexion and softness and smoothness never changed… maybe even improved. Carmella squinted her eyes and tried to remember the last time she saw Aunt Clara with make-up… *any kind... rouge… lip stick…* the answer was… *Never..!!! Never once!! All these years… and look at how soft and smooth her skin looks tonight with the cold January night air causing it to blush a bit… beautiful!!* Carmella thought, *Aunt Clara will always be cute… even in her old age… that childhood innocence of cuteness… especially with that little turned up button nose.*

Elvira always thought that Aunt Clara's eyes were sad, and it often made her feel melancholy. Elvira thought her eyes were sad, even when she smiled. A mental picture crossed Elvira's mind, the day she visited her aunt and had told her that the doctors were checking her breast for cancer. They were awaiting the results of a test.

Aunt Clara had leaned forward, reached across the kitchen table and gently put her hands on Elvira's forearms, squeezed them a bit and said… "No, no you worry, pray to the Blessed Madonna… believe in Her… I'll a pray for you too… yule a get better." Elvira smiled when she remembered that that was eight years ago.

Marie Delores's face lit up when her aunt entered the room and she smiled that beautiful smile, which could tell a perfect stranger... *nice to see you... yes.... we, you and I, are safe... you are welcomed and loved... come, I am happy to see you!* And Marie Delores thought of the time her oldest child, a daughter, (Marie Delores, born after five sons) was moving to North Carolina; her son-in-law's plant had been sold to a conglomerate and only a specific few were offered a transfer and a position. The kid didn't like it... *but whatz he gunna do... dare's no work here in Utica... not at that salary anyway... whatz he gunna do?? He's gotta go! La Distina-La fortuna...* (their destiny, their luck). Both went to Aunt Clara's flat, the daughter to say good-bye, to show proper respect and ask for Aunt Clara's blessings.

Marie Delores remembers that morning; her daughter did indeed get Aunt Clara's heartfelt and sincere blessings and both received some advice. "Itza gunna be hard for you Marie... but you gotta be strong, don't show a sad face to your daughter or enabee else... and yule-a, yule-a gotta call youra momma ebreyr week...and come home for Christmas... youa gotta be strong, in front of you husband... na sadda face... the boya gotta do whatza best for eberee body... yule a and da kids gotta help him." And then, Marie Delores and her daughter kissed Aunt Clara... and her great aunt added, "Mea pray for you and youra family yulea be-a happy... cum and see me again."

Linda and Rita, the youngest of the girls, got up quickly and went to their aunt's side; both helped the older woman take off her heavy coat. Rita scurried to the bedroom and gently creased the coat and laid it on the bed. She deliberately took the time to place the kerchief in one of the sleeves of the coat. Linda took her chair and moved it closer to the kitchen table and by the furnace register... (it was a cold night) and offered it to Aunt Clara... She then placed Rita's chair next to it. It did not remain vacant for long.

It seemed all of the sisters offered Zia Clara coffee and food at the same time, but Aunt Clara only replied, "Just coffee for now." Presto… there it was!! "You sure Aunt Clara, you don't want anything else...?" "…Naw naw… dis abee enuff."

Teresa, the eldest, caught DeeBee's eye and with a quick jerk of head… to the right toward where Aunt Clara was sitting… signaled DeeBee to be first to go and pay their respects to the newly crowned matriarch. DeeBee nodded to Tree… that nod that showed and told… *yes I know… of course I know!!!* …he then looked at Sam and without saying anything to him, told him he should follow when he was done. Sammy too, knew… *yes I know… of course I know!!!* …took a little sip of his Black Velvet and water, and dutifully awaited his turn.

All the 'Kids'… Tony, Donetta and her sister, Tony's brothers, Aunt Lucy's children… now all adults… always called their aunts… *Zist*, a bastardization of Zia. Further the

kids Americanized the word 'uncle' to pronounce it *Zee* in lieu of Zio. Even to this day *Zist* and *Zee* emerge in conversations. DeeBee left his chair at the table and went and sat in the empty chair next to Aunt Clara.

"How are you Zist??" A reply… "Ay-ya Ant-'nee… howza you daughter?"

What a mind on this woman, DeeBee thought… *his daughter her tonsils removed two weeks ago and she remembered.* "She's okay, she's doing fine, how is Tony?"

"He iz-ah good, heiz-ah cumma for-a the funeral. Ebre ding okay for you Anda-Knee?" "Yeah, Zist, everything is all right, Ma is at peace now and is resting." "Yessa dat's right, you are a good boy… a good boy" (she repeated), and then she leaned slightly forward and offered Dee Bee her cheek. He kissed her and his eyes went watery. DeeBee got up off of the chair and big Sammy sat and said "How are you, Zist?"

Zia Lucia's girls followed in the order of birth years… a matter of respect… of respect and honor. As the night progressed and others came to express their condolences, the old kitchen took on a festive and party atmosphere. Anybody who knew Zia Lucia knew that this is what she would want, a party… laughing, food and above all… *la famiglia*… the family. Yes, Zia Lucia would very much want that.

Trampoline

Pg Dn

It was late afternoon, and Tony was feeling tired: again. He thought *is this old age???? ...is my body telling me something??? ...is this a sign?? ...the start of the beginning of the end?? You ain't no spring chicken... always tired and you didn't do nuttin... tired!* He took another sip of wine, then lifted the glass to eye level and tried to see if he could make out the bird bath through the Chianti. Just vaguely. *Gotta change that water in the birdbath... looks scummy... ah heck!! ...later... I'll do it later.*

He put his stemmed wine glass down on the screen porch table and noticed the base of the glass had created a red circle. *Gotta wipe that up... it'll stain for sure... you know how wine is...* he studied the red circle and it made him remember something... something way, way back and he said aloud, "Ring around the rosie, a pocket full pocket full of posie..."

After July 28th, 1928

It was the middle of August, shortly after she came to America, Ma and her sisters and her sister-in-law all chipped in and bought twelve bushels of tomatoes, three for each family. Zia Grazia negotiated a deal with Nick the Farmer... if she ordered twelve bushels she could "Jew him down" to paying for only ten. The tomatoes were beautiful... big... red... ripe... solid shoulders and few if any water cracks. They were to be canned and stored in the cellars and used once the fresh tomatoes were no longer available in the market and in stores. You "gotta" have at least three quarts every Sunday, to make enough for the big Sunday dinner sauce, enough for left over macaroni sauce for Tuesday and still enough for left-left over sauce for Thursday. The sauces got progressively weaker... and more meatless... as the week progressed. That is why Sunday's sauce was the most plentiful, best and *freshest.*

Everybody in the neighborhood knew that Tuesdays and Thursdays were macaroni nights. Even Coach Phil Hammes knew that Tuesday and Thursdays were macaroni nights, it coincided with his 'live scrimmage' days at football practice; faithfully *live scrimmages* Tuesdays, Wednesdays and Thursdays. Often during Thursday night scrimmages Coach Hammes would say something like "comma you guys, hit harder… tonight is macaroni night and you got a dish waiting at home." The coach was a funny guy when he wanted to be.

First it was Salvatore, then Angelo and finally Tony who came home after practice and tiredly climbed the sixteen steps up the rear staircase to the second floor flat. And, the macaroni was always good… it stuck to your ribs… and if you were lucky, maybe meatballs and a piece of hot sausage… if you were lucky.

That was to come for Ma's three sons, however; now and this coming fall, she would have two going to Brandegee (class 6B and class 4B) and young Tony was to start in kindergarten. The older boys went bean picking that morning under the watchful eyes of Lucy and Carmella.

The other older cousins, Donnetta, Teresa, Frances and Ro, were delegated many duties at home that day; the easiest of which was watching the younger children, Tony, Joey, DeeBee and Little Sammy, as well as Mary Frances and Linda and still another, little Anthony. This assignment was easy because *watchmen* could station themselves at the mouth of the alleyway and far enough away from the back porch stoop to jump rope and maybe play hopscotch. Teresa didn't get her *own* jacks yet, but she still wanted them. The young ones were corralled in between the garbage shanty and fence in the backyard, and the canyon created by the three story, red brick wall of Tony's brownstone tenement house. Goomba Nicolo's two story frame, with its peaked roof, and the *gate* (the street entrance of the alley) was guarded by the big cousins. An eight foot wide and maybe fifty feet long strip that God also watched from above, just as the older cousins guarded at ground level.

The older girls worked in pairs. They would alternate, two would stay at the mouth of the canyon and the other pair would help in Zia Grazia's kitchen. The four stout matriarchs were peeling the skin from the tomatoes, discarding the skins into a *menassa* (garbage) bowl, and the juicy and soggy tomato pulp into canning quarts. The canning jars were made of glass, had *Ball* inscribed in script on it, and had a separate glass lid that would be secured only after the rubber ring jar lid was properly placed. The canning jars had a metal, thick-gauge wire hinged to the jar with an arm or clasp going over the lid and the other clamped down onto the quart itself.

One of the mothers would always be by the big speckled blue and white kettle on the range. The women were going to try and get all twelve bushels done today. The bounty would be divided by four.

The dreaded working detail for the girls consisted of washing canning jars and taking out the tomato skins and stems. The 'waste', the stems and peels, was placed in a large macaroni pot and the two girls would each get one of the handles and carry the filled pot down the second floor front stairs of the brownstone, across Catherine Street, to Zia Lucia's backyard, to dump and spread the contents around Zio Sarafino's little garden. The widow landlady of Zia Lucia allowed Zio Sarafino to plant there, without ever saying so but expecting a percentage of the crop for her table. The young girls would always change hands before crossing the street, the pot handle would kind of cut into their palms and leave a red mark on their hands and sometimes it would take a long time to rub it out, and another thing, it would hurt!

Donnette and Frances secretly wished and then even shared their hope that when they returned the empty large kettle, one of the four matriarchs upstairs in Zia Grazia's flat would tell them to switch with the other two, Teresa and Lucy. *God, I hope so!!*

"Okay… go tell Teresa and Lucy to come here now…"

Their wish was granted. And somehow they were rejuvenated… not at all tired from *all that work* they had been subjected to earlier. They could not get down the front stairs fast enough to assume the duty of watching the front of the canyon made by the alleyway. "Ma wants youse upstairs now!!"

It would be ridiculous to think the latter team assumed the changing of their responsibilities without a little, maybe a lot, of grumbling but fair is fair and further, *Ma sez so!!!* Antoinette and Fran had earlier left their skip rope and a piece of borrowed white blackboard chalk from Brandegee School (*I'll bring it back when we go back to school in September… maybe*). The piece of old clothes line rope for friendly competition, the chalk for a hopscotch grid…. Teresa and Lucy didn't draw their grids as nice as Fran could.

Shortly after the girls established their watch, Tony and DeeBee came to them and said they were all *sooo* thirsty and asked permission to go to Tony's flat to get a glass of water to drink. Joey and little Sammy were thirsty too. "Okay but don't break nuttin and come right down when you are done." Fran and Donnette unraveled their skipping ropes, properly distanced themselves from one another and, almost as if on cue, started: *My mother gave me a nickel to buy a pickle… I didn't buy a pickle…*

The four young boys heard them from afar starting up the chant, secretly giggled and climbed the rear staircase to Tony's flat. *Wonder what ever happened to the third spindle in the banister.* Nobody was thirsty. The ulterior motive for the sortie upstairs was to use Tony's double bed as a trampoline. They had done it before but never, never when Ma was around… "if Ma knew or found out about it… she'd kill ya dead…" they made a point of always straightening out the bedspread when they were done.

The bouncing action started out moderate enough, one at a time, but then escalated to two, three, and finally four boys at once. The boys held hands and did "ring around the rosie" and they all fell down in an eruption of hearty laughter. Little Sammy got to giggling and laughing so much, it weakened him, and compounded by the sponginess of the mattress, it made him collapse every time he tried to stand. And that made him giggle even more. It was contagious; the other three boys soon got as silly as little Sammy.

Ring around the rosie… a pocket full of posie… ashes ashes… we all fall down!!

They would fall on their behinds, with their backs on the mattress and their legs and feet above their heads. Laughing… having a grand time; it had to end. 'Okay that's enough," Tony ordered, "we gotta fix the bedspread and go back down stairs. Don't tell anybody!!" The latter order was for little Sammy, because he was the youngest, he had to be properly trained in the rules and regulations of BOYS of Catherine Street.

They all went downstairs and sat on the rear stoop and little Sammy was still giggling uncontrollably. *Whadda great afternoon that was!!!*

Pg Dn

Tony looked at the circle wine stain on the glass table top… *aye, you zoned out again… ya gotta wipe it up…* and as he did it he recited the old nursery rhyme aloud. In his adulthood he came to find out that that nursery rhyme came about from some kind of plague in Ole England. The ring around the rosie, as he remembers it now, was a sore that would eventually get infected and a pocket full of posie, was the puss bag that formed and the ashes ashes… was the pallor of the victim and… we all fall down was death.

SHIT!! Who sez the truth don't hurt?? Or a little knowledge is a dangerous thing?? What an ugly picture for such a simple, child's carefree nursery rhyme… It'll never be the same to me. How could it?

The stain is gone now. Tony thought, I liked it a whole lot better when I thought a ring around the rosie was a circle around a rose and holding hands and dancing around it and a pocket full of posie, in young Tony's world, was rose petals in your pocket and the ashes, ashes and we all fall down was when Pa banked the firebox in that big old black stove and then shook the bottom grate… and the ashes would all fall down… creating a little dust cloud above the receptacle. And he remembered Sammy, DeeBee and Joey and all that laughter.

Tony could see where the wording of the lyrics could be justified, but maybe it was the wine he had consumed, he certainly like his interpretation much, much better.

We All Fall Down

I am a reasonable man

    I am a reasonable man... always was... Why back in the old days when I sold wholesale and maybe some protection... I was always fair... always...

    Whenever an ambitious greenhorn opened or started a business... bakery... meat market... pork store... haberdashery... trucking... whatever....I always gave them maybe a year or two... always... I never stifled them or poisoned growth in the early years of getting it together... never...

    When they were up and running... I sold them what I had in the wholesale store and maybe some protection against the crooked cops and those Irish American kids that preyed on some of the greenhorns... and maybe sometimes even helped them collect debts that others owed them (for a reasonable percentage)... always a reasonable man... do you hear me God... always fair... You do hear me, don't you, Lord God??? God?? Are you listening?? I feel I helped them... I still think I helped them.

    The tough baker way over on the east side??? Oh, that!!! That was a long time ago... You heard of him? ...bad scene... the out of town package... got a little too carried away... maybe the gasoline was going too far... but... how was I to know that he got a big shipment that morning??? I didn't wanna break him... but... it happened... successa... you, know God, after that incident, God... the cost of those outside packages became very, very expensive... some connections just outright refused to come... are you angry at me, Lord?? I tried to be a fair man... I had intended on only selling him the normal protection like the other merchants and business people... What?? What was it?? Five dollars for each one hundred pound sack of flour purchased... maybe it came out to be couple of pennies... not more than a nickel a loaf...

it was for his own good… he could just as well have been hurt by those ruffians we protected him from… we did him a serv...

Don Salvatore never finished the thought or the sentence or the word, he knew that God was smirking at him for using the word 'protection' and his 'reasonableness' no longer sounds true, not even to him.

"A volpe cambia la, pelle ma non il vizio."
(A fox will change his fur, but not his habits.)

The train pulled into Yonkers. The package got off, two men supporting the one with a badly swollen face. They brought the young man to a hospital, a small one nearby… it was called St. Mary's House of Refuge. The nephew remained unconscious; the doctor on duty could not tell them if he was going to be all right. The uncle had to tell his sister… had to tell her something… he had to! But what and how… *Oh shit, oh shit, whadda lousy mess… that bastard wouldn't go down… he probably permanentely messed up the kid's face… hope he'll be all right… God I hope so… Whadda am I gunna tell Josie… Whadda am I gunna tell her??... the three of us… for a lousy hundred bucks… oh shit, whadda am I gunna tell her??*

After that special package trip to Utica (that little piece of cake job), those that knew the uncle all noticed he became much more reckless, much more dangerous to himself and those around him. They started to call him Crazy Horse. Three years later, he was found shot, three bullets to the back of the head. He was found in a restaurant alleyway behind four Wheeling, West Virginia garbage cans. The investigating cops and detectives thought they smelled gasoline and only speculated as to why but warned all new arrivals at the scene not to smoke.

Chiudere l'occhi e bevi l'aceto…
(Close your eyes and drink the vinegar)

The third party of the trio relived that smash to his chest at least once a day for the rest of his life. He tried to find the reason at the bottom of every whiskey bottle, wine bottle and beer bottle he came across. He ended up in a

Salvation Army Mission house; alone and penniless. They found him dead in a dirty little restroom of an abandoned gas station. The restroom still smelled of gasoline.

Che pesce si???
(What kind of fish are you???)

The boy with the broken face never totally regained his senses or for that matter consciousness. His mother never again spoke to her brother and shunned every gesture or act of kindness he tried to give. The boy ended up in an earlier version, or attempt, of a rehab house, deep in the Bronx by Spanish Harlem. His mother would visit every Wednesday, leaving her home early in the morning and coming home after dark. She would take him a bowl of soup; it was easier to feed him soup that she made the night before. What she hated the most was seeing her beautiful son always drooling. The woman would quietly cry all the way home on the train ride, sometimes looking at, but not seeing her reflection in the glass.

On one such Wednesday night, traveling home on the subway from the 'rehab center', his mother, alone in her sorrowful thoughts and tears quietly running down her cheeks... looking out the window, her nostrils suddenly tweaked and flailed, *where was that smell of gas coming from???* A passenger, just two seats up, rose and moved toward the exit door. She noticed that the fellow passenger had on a blue waist coat... in time they would be called Eisenhower jackets... and on his chest, right beneath his left shoulder was an emblem, the logo for Mobil Gas... a flying red horse. Her son passed on that night at three forty-five a.m.

Sette ha fatto a mammata... ma tu sei apui bella!!!

(Your mother made seven... but... you... you are the most beautiful!!!)

That night, so long ago, when a baseball bat shattered an oven peel, seemed lost in the darkness of all the sins of the past: a black pool in the back of your mind that you avoided and only peered into when forced by something. Agatha and John had stopped at DeVito's bakery near the church right after the seven-thirty mass. The bakery was located on Sacco and Vanzetti Streets in Endicott, New York. They wanted to purchase a couple of loaves of fresh-hot Italian bread for their Sunday dinner and the company.

The kids, their kids and… all the grand kids… were coming over for Sunday dinner and to belatedly celebrate his sixtieth birthday, it fell on Thursday this year. They were going to have a house full and he thought to himself… *I am truly blessed.* Agatha never really knew why and because of her husband's temper, she wisely, never really pursued a logical reason why they left Utica that cold February so many years ago. He came home earlier in the morning and just went to bed. She knew he didn't sleep, but tossed and turned for the longest time. When he got out of bed, he started to drink a bottle of whiskey. He remained morose, moody and distant… *no, not the time to ask questions…* Agatha was a wise woman. By Saturday of that week, John had quit his truck driving job with Don Salvatore wholesalers, withdrew their savings from the Perretta Bank and with his wife and his young son boarded the 13:45 D & L train to Endicott. His cousins got him a job at a shoe factory the next week. John did well at the factory and eventually became a foreman. Agatha liked it there and was once again happy and bore John another son and a beautiful little girl with a smile that even the angels of heaven could have had trouble matching.

His daughter loved to skip rope and reminded John of somebody out of his past... but he could not ever really remember who or where or when... but somebody he used to know or knew of... whatever. There were several customers in the bakery, and John and Agatha took their place in line. John casually looked to the right of the crowded bread counter and noticed the door to the rear baking room was wedged open and the help was scurrying in and out of the two rooms. On the very far right, he saw a neatly piled stack of hundred pound flour bags, three bags lay east/west, one bag north/south and the next tier would alternate. John blinked... *NO, NO, don't go there, no...* he remembered as a young boy running and chasing after his brothers in the mountains of and stopping suddenly and looking down at the ravine and becoming very frightened... looking down into that abyss... *no, no, don't go there...*

He shook his head and quickly looked away from the paper flour sacks, in the old days they were made of unbleached cloth, *focus on something else, anything.* As the fates would have it, he slowly turned to the oven and watched the baker insert and then quickly retrieve the peel which was on a long handle. He propped the peel vertically against the oven for a second to give his assistant a hand in moving a large wooden proof box with eight long drawers. The baker stretched his long arms pulling the proofer by two black handles and his assistant, with his shoulder to the proofer, was pushing... John looked back at the baker's long arms... *No, NO, NO, NO, don't go there... running the ravine, the abyss... you are going to fall into the ravine... the deep steep ravine...*

John shut his eye lids as firmly as he could, shook his head violently; then forced his eyes open. His eyes eventually focused on the wooden peel resting against the oven wall. John became very quiet... he no longer even blinked... he became very quiet. He felt his chest rising and falling as he breathed, he smelled the wholesome odor of bread baking... he wasn't in this world, he was....

"John?? JOHN... John, are you all right?? Are you all right???" poor Agatha was almost panicking at the sight of her husband... she had never seen him so pale, so... sorrowful... "John??? John... per l'amour di Dio (for the love of God) what is wrong!!" What seemed like an eternity to Agatha, which is so often the case in a panicked situation, John slowly closed his eyes, opened them, and quietly whispered in his wife 's ear, "I'm okay... just a little dizzy... I'll go wait in the car..."

"John... are you sure you are all right..." good wives have a special sense and she looked closely into his face, especially his eyes. He smiled weakly and answered... "Yeah Aggie... I'm okay... I'll be all right... get the bread... I'll wait in the car... you got enough money for the bread??"

She continued to look deep into his face for another minute and she only nodded her reply. John left the bakery and went to his vehicle, it was parked too far away and he knew his wife's eyes were on him all the way to the car door. She looked away after he got behind the steering wheel. John gripped the wheel as tightly as he could, he suppressed the urge to vomit... he remembered vomit splattering on the bakery floor... the mixed odor of bread cooking and vomit... and... what??? ...gasoline?? So way far away... a zillion years ago. He did not vomit. He wept as he never wept before and his head went from side to side... his eyes closed tightly.

The car's rear door opened and Agatha placed the six loaves of bread on the back seat, two loaves for each of the kids to take home after the Sunday dinner. John knew she saw him crying, but he could not stop. She got into the passenger side of the vehicle and placed her purse on her lap and sat silently. John regained his composure, sniffed three or four times and blew his nose and started the car. Agatha did not say anything, it was John who quietly reassured her and said, "I'm all right".

Agatha remained silent. Agatha was a very wise and understanding person. She did, however, in her own thoughts recite a prayer the nuns taught her in sister school: "Oh my Jesus forgive us our sins, lead all souls to heaven, especially those of us who have most need of your mercy." She silently recited that prayer all the way home, and she had recited it not only for her husband, but for herself and for every one who caused her husband such sorrow… and guilt.

Agatha was a very wise and understanding soul. She knew that in an old house there is never a lack for bad memories.

Alla casa vecchia non mangano I surgi….
In an old house there
is never a lack of rats…

The sinners among us

Two black kids, Jimmy 'The Big M' and Clarence aka CeeBee, and three white kids, Joey Del, Pokey Mike and Johnny Brains... all between thirteen and fourteen... skipped school in Boston that day. They had long ago eaten their lunches... while walking to the park. When they got to the park, they didn't do much... sat on the park benches... threw flat stones... side arm... into the creek and watched them skip along the surface... and just hung out. "*Hey, keep an eye out for Mrs. Sisti's* (the school truant officer) *black De Soto... if we get caught we'll be in a shit load of trouble!!!*"

At about noon time they decided to pool their money, walk about twenty blocks downtown and go to a movie theater. They had a lot of time to catch the matinee. As usual CeeBee & Joey Del didn't have enough money, but the others were able to cover the cost of the admission. They caught a double feature and still got out too early to go home. "Lets go to the old (now abandoned) cloth mill and throw rocks at the rats... we gotta lotta time!!!"

The boys did just that. They picked up some rocks by the old railroad side of the factory by the loading dock and practiced a bit of their 'rat killer throws'. Because it wasn't late enough (the rats usually came out at or after dusk), there was no rat activity. "Let's turn over sum of dat junk piled up against the wall over dare.... see if we can scare sum fat rat out."

Pokey Mike lifted a big piece of tar paper that covered about half of the pile of junk. Pokey quickly raised his right arm behind his ear, a stone clutched in his fist, and so did all the other boys; they were ready to fire their *rat killer throw.*

Five pairs of eyes quickly scanned the unmasked surface, listening for the scurrying sounds and looking for the quick motion of a fleeing rat with it long, thick, ugly tail. Nothing. A second or two later, after the disappointing no show of the rat or rats… they all said almost simultaneously, "Holy Shit!!!" They were all frightened and startled by what they saw, some more frightened than others. Johnny Brains half whispered half hissed, "Let's get the hell outta 'ear."

They all ran and this time Pokey Mike actually led the pack. The boys ran just on the side of the old railroad tracks, to the end of the old long factory building, and made a quick (leaning hard to the left) right turn down the alleyway, the canal to their backs, to the safety of Prince Street. Finally, they stopped to catch their breaths.

It was Big M who first saw the beat cop near the fruit stand and said to the group, "Should we tell him???" A pause followed, the boys looked at one another… "Can we git in trouble, my fadder'll kill me!!… why not… we ain't don nuttin wrong… lets do it!!!

It's the right thing to do… OKAY… Let's do it!!"

They told Officer Schmidt. He looked at them and said, "Ya sure!!" "Yes!!! Yes!!! We're positive!!!" "Okay, show me." Three of the boys didn't want to go with Officer Schmidt, but he said sternly… "All of ya gotta come." They all went.

When they got there, Officer Schmidt of Boston's finest, saw the final resting place of Alberino. His right leg was barefooted and without a sock, his left trouser leg was ripped and you could easily see Alberino's scrawny knee, but what was most repulsive… two boys vomited looking at it for the second time, was that the rats had already started eating away at the flesh of his face. Officer Schmidt… maybe because he had three boys of his own… said to the shocked boys, "You kids go home now…" and added "forget about it, he was probably just a bum." Officer Schmidt called in the report…

... Charley Stubbs was a black man, who worked hard and had a fistful of dreams. His wife and his family were the world to him. Eventually and with their help, he achieved some of those dreams, a place out in the country, riding horses (only two) and his own business, a nursing home for the elderly, and two of his four kids in college.

However, at this point in time, Charlie is a much younger man, going to school during the day, nursing school, and working at the State Hospital in Boston, near the docks. He had recently been promoted to 'night supervisor'... six days on... three days off. He was doing well and would continue to do well.

Shortly after he took over the Eighth Ward, on the third floor rear section of the building, he made the discovery that his predecessor had inadvertently destroyed or lost a file on one of the older patients in his ward. It came about that a week or so before his predecessor relocated to Worcester, she had had the file out on her desk and... they speculate... it got mixed up with the daily newspaper... right there in the left hand corner... and was accidentally brought down to the incinerator. The patient who occupied the third bed... from the east side door in a long row of ten beds... under one of the four windows in the ward... soon became know as Missy Mom. Missey Mom was Charlie's grandmother's name and because of Missey Mom's pure white hair and... not very pretty... toothless mouth... the patient on the third floor was so named by Charlie... a little remembrance of his beloved grandmother. Charlie had two sections of twenty beds to supervise with only two assistants, if they showed for work that day.

Charlie started a new file on Missey Mom and made a special note therein alerting the future caregivers that during a thunder storm she had a tendency to become violent and very frightened... she will not... definitely not eat green string beans... she will fold her arms over her chest and keep repeating in both English and, I think, Italian, "...no, you did not hurt me… no, you did not hurt me…" and sometimes "…you have got to go now…" and she'll keep repeating "…you have to go now."

Charlie, with all his blessings, was also a very a sensitive man. He learned a lot by watching his little, frail, white grandmother. Although many of his staff members and those on the day trick, found 'Missey Mom' a gold mine 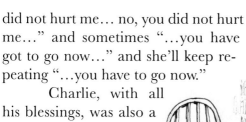 of funny stories and jokes… "she was a nutso, you know…. why the hell else would she be in here?" …he saw a small, troubled person with a lot of mental pain and anguish.

One night, in April, a thunder storm came rolling out of the Berkshire Mountains and headed for Boston; before it was over, it had deposited a half inch of rain in less than an hour. On the third floor rear, of the State Hospital, the Eighth Ward… most of the patients slept. To those few who were awake, they merely accepted the roaring and crashing thunder, the wind rattling the four windows and old Annie's screaming and crying. One of Charlie's assistants did hear her above the natural roars of Mother Nature and got up to get the leather belt restraints. Charlie saw him do so and quietly asked, "Those for Missey Moms?"

The attendant replied, "You betchca… listen to that crazy looney, she's gonna wake up all the other wards."

Charlie just waved him off with a hand gesture and said, "Let me handle it." Charlie was a big man and always spoke deliberately and at a pitch that forced a listener to concentrate. He had a darker hue which made his ivory white teeth even brighter than normal and when he smiled it was reassuring to most.

"You need any help?" his assistant asked.

"Naw… tanks… it'sa piece of cake." He walked into the bay area to attend to that little old woman that reminded him of his grandmother… his white grandmother. He found Annie X wide-eyed and frightened and thrashing in her little iron framed... painted white… hospital cot. "Missey… Missey… Missey… it's okay… it'll be over soon… soon."

As he quietly spoke to her, he reached over the bed and found her small frail arms and gently but firmly pressed her elbows to the thin mattress. "It's okay… it's okay… it'll be over soon." He genuinely smiled at this poor little creature that probably didn't once, in her whole life, hurt someone… anyone! She thrashed her legs, but with her upper body restricted gently at the arms, her strength lessened. Charlie noticed how very, very thin her legs were… she had kicked off the sheet of her cot.

Then she was quiet. Her eyes, no longer unblinking and wide open and staring at something in the ceiling; but becoming softer as her eyelids slowly covered them and they opened again. She was breathing normally now. Charlie released his grip from her elbows and almost before his arms reached his side, Missey Moms had her arms crisscrossed over her breast. She was smiling now and her eyes remained closed. Then she said, "No you didn't hurt me… you did not hurt me…" a few second later she said, "You have to go now… no, you didn't hurt me… you have to go now."

Charlie, the night supervisor of the Eighth Ward at the state Hospital, looked down at the little old lady that reminded him so much of his old grandmother and especially when she was dying, reached down and fixed the bed sheets she had kicked off herself earlier. The big gentle man then reached down with the back of his left hand and slowly and lovingly pushed the strand of white hair from her cheeks. It had flopped down there during her ordeal with insanity.

Charlie heard her say again as he was leaving the bay area, "No... You didn't hurt me... you did not hurt me...." a slight pause and then, "you have got to go now... you have got to go now..." When Charlie got back to his desk to finally complete some of those forms, he could not help thinking to himself, that little Missey Mom was not really talking to him about not hurting her and you had to go... no... he was pretty sure she was talking to somebody else.

That night, Alberino's second wife, Anna Maria died in her sleep. And nobody even knew her real name.

Fa beni e scorda.
(Do good and forget it.)

Fa mali e ricorda.
(Do bad and remember.)

Zia Minucca

Pg Dn

When Tony was in the army and stationed in Germany, he went to Italy for the first time. At the time, it was one of the highlights of his life... even today he fondly remembers a slew of pleasant thoughts and can easily re-run the lasting images imprinted in his mind. It was then, the first time he went, that he met Zia Carmella, quick as ever, even in her old age, but still, quiet... reserved... *'liking it'* in the shadows of others... she herself a shadow... willing and ready to serve. She did, however, show some signs of old age. And then, Tony went back to the old country... some ten years later.

This time he went with his wife, as he was to do many more times in the future and it was as good as before. Maybe from then on, he 'saw' Italy as an adult and not as a youth.

The Adriatic was as blue and serene as ever with little white puffs of clouds drifting lazily by... peaceful... The family was all well but still mourning the passing of Zia Maria Nicole three years back. Zia Carmella was now living with her oldest niece, Maria Nicole's spinster daughter, Lizzetta. They shared a room in Michelini's new home in the country. Niece and aunt maintained the household, cleaning and cooking and washing clothes and watching the children. They still attended mass daily at the old Church of the Ascension in town: on rainy days they took the early bus. In time, however, Lizzetta's duties increased and Zia Minucca's (Carmella's) duties steadily decreased, but to all concerned and in testament to their character and ethics... no complaint was ever voiced.

Shortly after Tony and his wife arrived, Michelini's (one of his first cousins), family had a big spread and invited all the relatives to come to meet their new American cousin with beautiful blond hair. The younger children almost rudely stared at her... wide eyed and not blinking... those a bit older asked permission to just touch it. They were awed, only in the movies, and recently television, did they see yellow hair.

The table was a cornucopia of food... Tony shook his head in wonderment and believed that no one could put another glass or bottle on the table's surface... but they did. If they needed room, they'd move or replace. It was a very large and spacious kitchen and dining area. There was a small, quaint old-fashioned and seldom used fireplace in one of the corners of the room. It was used on special occasions and more for show: the serious cooking was done in an adjacent table-less kitchen area. Today the fireplace was used to roast chestnuts and the chestnuts had the same little "X's" carved into them with a pointed knife... like they did in East Utica. Zia Minucca sat on a small stool, off to the left and quietly witnessed the unending feast.

The men at the table soon loosened their belts and/or waistbands and took turns sighing. There were deep and contented sighs, and the wine, espresso and the sambuco were all so very, very good. From Tony's vantage point, near the head of the table and slightly to his right, he could see Zia Minucca sitting there. Like a shadow on the wall... a ghost of times past... a witness to a thousand such feasts... No... No... not a ghost... more of a small statue of a holy grandmother... a saint. *Watch the wine!!! Tony... watch the wine!! You drink too much!!*

Tony's head was cocked a bit and his eyes slowly hooded as he studied her. She is toothless now... refusing expensive dental work in her old age... if you'd ask her why... she'd say something like... "God wants a clean soul and a kind heart and He doesn't worry about faces"... (*watch the wine Tony... watch the wine*) ...her face is wrinkled... her eyes deeply set... there are little hairs coming out of her ears... she wheezes a bit when she breathes... and seems to smile at nothing... *You are old, Zia Minucca... you are very old...*

but you beat 'em !!! YOU beat them all!!! All of them bastards...
ALL of 'EM!!! Tomasino and Nicolo and Pasqual and Frank
Vendora, all of them...and you beat 'em by thirty - forty years...
you did it!! You did it, Kid... Bravo!!! (Yeah!!... I know... Doctor
Rossi said she is not long for this world... not long at all.)

The next time Tony and his wife visited the old
country, Zia Minucca had passed on. They showed him a
photograph of her seated by that picturesque domed corner
fireplace with a huge cake in front of her... and only three
lit candles... one each for the past... the present... and...
the future. She was ninety-six years old.

To The Victors....

It has been twenty days since Alberino and his wife disappeared. At their nine-o-six espresso meeting, Mr. Sabitano broached the subject at hand. There appeared to be two excellent opportunities regarding the pending future of the old converted horse barn, with that small apartment in the old loft and its only entrance a rickety, exposed staircase at the rear of the structure. The last occupant was a bakery.

Don Salvatore was considering buying it for a warehouse for his ever growing wholesale food business... plus there was some talk of prohibition. The other prospect was Carmine Romano, the Calabrese, an electrician who had just finished paying off the mortgage on his house. He had been running his business out of his home and was doing well. Two of his three sons were learning the trade and there was a lot of work around town... ripping out old gas lines... and wiring the old homes... plus there were new homes going up... but their biggest prize... was the retainer they got for servicing and maintaining the electricity at the Mohawk Textile Mill.

Don Salvatore could pay cash for the structure and Mr. Perretta was favoring the quick sale, to settle with the owner in Pescara and move on. Aldo Sabitano reasoned the bank should buy the house from the man in Pescara... The wiser selection was the Calabrese... he was a hard worker... he proved he could make payments... his son was to be married in September or August and he had to live somewhere... the Calabrese had a sweetheart of a deal with his supplier that if he could triple his monthly orders... store the supplies until needed... he could save a bushel basket of money... it was economics... in another thought... Aldo reminded Mr. Perretta of the proximity of the textile mills and the Canal and the sewer rats. Won't a food storage warehouse attract rats... isn't the community arming itself with cats? Every house seems to have cats... in the tenement houses the landlords don't want dogs... but welcome cats... they get fat on the sewer rats running around the neighborhood.

'Rats' was the buzz word; Aldo knew of Mr. Perretta's phobia of rats. He had studied the history of the bubonic plaque... it started in Sicily... tiny little fleas... so much death, so much devastation... no... no rats... ever!!

Notwithstanding Aldo's obvious overkill, he is convincing Mr. Perretta with the rat issue, the deal... the sale... with Carmine in the long run the better of the two. The Bank could easily satisfy the owner in Pescara (at a greatly reduced price... "who is going to buy that old barn???... down by the canal and those mills... we'd be lucky to find any kind of buyer... we'll probably lose money at any reasonable price asked...).

Mr. Perretta could be very convincing if motivated by profit. He already had an offer from Carmine, not quite as good as Don Salvatore's... but, as reliable and permanent... especially when the bank held the paper. The monthly payments would be there, the building occupied. The tenant would probably have a cat and the goods on the ground floor were not edible, nor attractive to rats. And... the money... The money... stays in the neighborhood and not in some downtown bank.

Aldo evaluated it just a tad differently; he was helping a man and his family get ahead... grow and prosper.

What about the material the former occupant abandoned?? Uncle Joe had an account at the bank and Zia Grazia was a frugal hands-on type of person... they could certainly use some of the equipment in the bakery. The little coal that is there, the three sacks of flour that Mr.

Griffin was supposed to pick up but never did… some peels and bread racks… see what it is worth to them… don't ever leave money on the table.

Uncle Joe… because of his… what??? …memories of the apartment… a longing… a wanting… a need for Anna Maria… did not attend the tour of the abandoned building and its offered material. "But Pepe… certainly there is some equipment you can use from the bakery… you can get it for pennies on the dollar… why not??"

"Let Grazia go, she knows what we can use or not use… and she'll drive a harder bargain than I can" and so, with this excuse, Uncle Joe was spared a sentimental journey to a place of once-lived warm and special memories… let them live in my heart and not torture my brain with its vision once more.

Zia Grazia gladly went in the truck with Enzo and little Michael and she got there early. Mr. Perretta and Mr. Sabitano were very impressed with Zia Grazia's bartering talent and her knowledge. Later they agreed that Pepe had nothing to worry about and was correct in his reason for not attending the walk through; she did well.

When they finished the walk through the abandoned bakery and Zia Grazia was about to settle accounts, she just happened to inquire if there was anything upstairs in the apartment. "Yes," they answered "…a little… but it isn't too good."

"Well, let me see… we not only have a bakery… we have an apartment and a big family too!!" They all climbed the rickety outside staircase and entered the abandoned apartment. Zia Grazia made a disgruntled sound as she looked around the small quarters and the old and very used furniture. She then lifted the curtain that acted as a door to the bedroom and stepped into the room. The bed was junk, she was about to turn and leave when she happened to spot the dome lid steamer truck that was once Alberino's first wife's pride and joy. It showed signs of heavy use and rough handling.

It took her breathe away... *steady... steady... don't show them your excitement... control... control... act the part...* she made an audible disgruntled sound and turned toward the doorway and started to leave the room. She slowed for a second and said over her shoulder... "I'll give you fifty cents for that dirty, beat up trunk... maybe we can use it in the bakery to keep some kettles or something...but it isn't worth anything more than fifty cents." Mr. Perretta nodded, and when her back was completely toward him, she smiled broadly.

The steamer truck was just like the one that her comarra in Italy had and used when she came to America with her family. Zia Grazia envied that family for such an attractive, sturdy and practical item. It had those fine leather straps to keep it firmly shut and its thick, strong leather grip-handles on either end to lift it, the brass corner guards and latches and the brass rivets holding the protective green painted tin sheeting and four wooden strips skids under it to help push it on flat surfaces. In her eyes, it was just beautiful... just beautiful. It had a tray that fitted neatly under the cover and into the chest about four inches... it had two circular holes on each end to enable you to easily

lift it in or out. It was beautiful… and now!!!… Grazia a Dio… she finally has her very own!

Enzo and Michael loaded the purchased material onto the back of the truck. She eyed them coming down the rickety stairs with the new found treasure and warned the boys to be careful and not fall… certainly not to fall with that treasure in their arms.

When they got back, she again supervised the carrying of the trunk into her apartment and immediately ordered two of her younger sisters to wash, clean, polish the brass, brush the leather inside and the tray. The girls worked hard and long, but the end result was spectacular, everyone in the household admired it.

Within a week, the trunk found a new home in Uncle Joe and Zia Grazia's bedroom. The bottom portion was filled with sheets and pillowcases and pure white table clothes and fine silks, the tray was mostly filled with important papers and documents and a cigar box. The key had long been lost, but you'd never really believe it because the brass center circular hinged lock and the brass latches were so highly polished and shined, you'd assume something so rich and fine was perfect… and it had a lock. A doily crocheted dress scarf was draped over the top and a bowl was placed in the center for decorative effect.

Uno per me, uno per te, e uno per il filgio de lo rei…

(One for me, one for you and one for the son of the king)

The Spoils of the Victors

It was a Thursday and Enzo had an exceptionally bad night. Luigi La Farina (La Farina being his nickname... few, if anybody, knew his surname) didn't show up last night to help at the bakery. Because Luigi La Farina was a bachelor and had a tendency to drink a lot, he was not too dependable, nor very dedicated to work. It was the second time this month he was a no-show. Uncle Joe knew all this, but hired him anyway because he was a baker, when sober, and since Alberino went missing, he had obtained more customers, and it was the time of the year when the bean pickers were in the fields. Everybody... especially the family members... worked harder and longer hours to keep up with the demand.

Enzo was in an exhausted frame of mind... exhausted from the monotony of rolling and shaping bread dough and filling drawers and drawers and covering them for a proofing or raising period; they used spilt halves of flour sacks to cover the raw bread and then closed the drawer of the eight tier gurney/truck. During this exhausted stage, he came down at nine o'clock last night and he and Uncle Joe made four batches. They were wrapping up the fourth one now... he kept repeating and repeating in his mind that little ditty they sang as children. A foolish little thing that just kept repeating and said, "One for me and one for you and one for the son of the king." He would occasional bob his head... catching himself doing touch and goes.

Uncle Joe told him, right after this batch, he was to go upstairs and wake Zia Grazia and young Michael... (she normally came down at eight in the morning to sell the bread and set up big orders... and young Michael would help)... but today it would have to be closer to seven. She would have to set up the big orders earlier and young Michael would help Uncle Joe bake that last batch of bread by carrying the loaves one at a time from the gurney drawers to the peel that Uncle Joe handled so efficiently.

Uncle Joe told him he should go upstairs and get a couple of hours sleep before making the delivery to some of the bean pickers shanties, those up by Deerfield and Holland Patent… a little closer than the southern run to Norwich and New Berlin. It was almost 6:00 AM when he woke Michael and told him to quietly wake Zia Grazia. Later, when the seven o'clock whistle blew, Zia Grazia would go back upstairs to wake up her younger sisters, for they too had to go to work at the mills and start by seven thirty. He would then return downstairs and continue preparing the big orders.

Enzo came downstairs briefly with Michael, just to get him situated in the routine of helping their big brother, and as he was leaving, he heard his sister-in-law tell her husband "…don't forget the flour delivery today… we are going to need fifty dollars for Mr. Griffin when he comes!!" Mr. Griffin now insisted on only cash from all the bakers, all the bakers, regardless of their past good payment record and reputation… everybody!!! This edict came about ever since Alberino stuck him for twenty dollars. Never again… everybody pays on delivery! Yes, Uncle Joe knew that!

Enzo went upstairs, stripped and flopped into the bed he shared with Michael, the sheets were still warm. He heard the seven o'clock whistle and just as he was drifting off to sleep, he heard Zia Grazia come upstairs and wake up the girls. They brought home a pay envelope, they worked, what did Enzo do?? …no pay envelope, but he ate three times a day like the girls. He was too tired to reason it out now, or like he had so many times before, dream of being rich like Govanni from West Virginia… a thousand dollars in his pocket. He fell asleep.

Uncle Joe shook Enzo's shoulder and Enzo came out of his slumber. "You okay?? You gotta get up now… it a little after ten o'clock… Michael will come with you… are you all right??" Enzo nodded yes, sat up and looked and found

his trousers, he hoisted them up and yawned. He was still tired but it was only up to Holland Patent today. He should be back by three… or three thirty. Uncle Joe told him to drink some strong coffee and wash his face to make sure he was totally awake. He washed first and then sat a moment to have a cup of the strong coffee which was made at six that morning. He patted his mustache and wondered if it really made him look older… if the girls in church thought he was twenty or twenty five. Like DiStefano who is now in Italy… they had *a thousand dollars* in their pocket when they came to Utica to get Minucca and they all went back to Italy.

The coffee was strong; he took a piece of hard bread and soaked a piece of it in the coffee. He fished it out with a spoon and dropped another one into the dark brew. He stretched a bit, got up and went back into the bedroom to get his hat.

He passed Uncle Joe's room and from the half opened door he saw his brother was kneeling by the open, domed steamer truck. He had his two hands in the upper tray and in the portion of the divided tray that had a lid. He took out a cigar box and opened it and took out some money. He was going to pay Mr. Griffin, the flour man. But Enzo had to make a delivery up in Holland Patent and Deerfield. Some people said he didn't work because he didn't bring home a pay envelope, he thought again; *what was work*.

He and Michael came back a little after 4:00 pm. He was still so very tired, he didn't even have any supper that night, but went immediately to bed. Michael followed right after he ate. When Enzo walked by his older brother's bedroom, the door was swung wide open, the bed was neatly made and the low rays of the sun came into the room from the window that faced the west. The fading sun light rested on and illuminated the dome steamer truck, and its brass fixtures, the latches, the circular hinged lock, the brass corner fixtures on each of the four floor corners, the over the dome straps (they were buckled), all taken in at one passing glance.

It was truly a treasure chest with a king's ransom in a Dutch Master Cigar box.

Enzo slept a long while and had to be shaken awake at four o'clock the next morning. Luigi La Farina came to work and Uncle Joe reprimanded him. Enzo was glad he came, it gave him time to rest and start to work at his normal hour... *but he didn't bring home a pay envelope.* The chest looked magnificent with the crochet doily and the blue glass bowl in the center.

Three weeks to the day, Zia Grazia went into her bedroom and gasped. Her beautiful domed steamer truck was opened wide... like a yawning hippo. The tray was resting on the edge, kitty-cornered, the tray lid was up and in the center of the divided tray was the Dutch Masters cigar box. She knew, yes, she knew even before she opened the cigar box, one of her brother-in-laws had come for his pay envelope. The ungrateful wrench, taking the flour money and her money, and maybe Uncle Joe's money. He took more than half of what they had left yesterday. She hissed her husband's name, and although he was in the kitchen, he detected the urgency and the foreboding tone of the hiss. He rushed to the room and when he entered... she merely extended herself to her tallest upright posture and pointed to the domed steamer truck. She would not ever again pray for her husband or any of his family members.

Uno per mei, uno per te, e uno per il figlio del rei...

(One for me one for you and one for the son of the king)

Pa's Turn

Pg Dn

He carefully eyed the liquid flowing out of the bottle and filling his wine glass. He twisted his wrist to make sure the last drop remained in the bottle and then stared a moment at the full glass. He put the bottle a little bit behind the ashtray and with the same hand picked up his Tuscany cigar, which he had just laid there before pouring the drink. It was still lit.

He smiled at the fact that it was still lit and he picked up his wine, took a sip… and didn't care one half of an iota that he was getting drunk. He bounced a bit on the chair that was part of the set of patio furniture he did not really like. *Okay Tony… so yur getting stoned, aye!! You are in one of those god damn moods where you know all the answers and can figure out any problem you want too!"* He leaned over, took another sip, swallowed and then took two puffs on his cigar. He liked to watch the bluish-gray smoke rise and after all these years, the smell doesn't bother him at all.

He looked down at his big stomach and then to his pillar-like thighs… *look at that stomach… look at those thighs… you can land a lousy god damn B-29 on 'em fur Christ Sakes!!!* He reminded himself that he wasn't too pretty anymore and then in the same breath remembered he *never was* too pretty. He leaned back and rolled his head, another good sign of a drunken stupor and yawned like a resting lion.

Whether he liked it or not, he was walking to the edge, that dreaded edge, he wanted to avoid it and really didn't want to go there. Some-thing was dragging at him… what was it… *Gotta be the wine… Fight it!!! Fight it!!! Don't go dare!!!*

Pg Up

... What??? Fifty-sixty years ago??? Ma's crying like crazy and Angelo's got her right arm and is pulling and Ma is clinging with a death like grip to the kneeler in front of Pa's casket... her fingers are turning white she is squeezing so hard. You are on the other side... "Come on Ma!!! Come on Ma!! We gotta go... Come on Ma... Please!!!"

She continued to wail... "God, Please I don't want this...!!! Please I don't want this!" One by one, you loosen those fingers... grab her palm hold it tight!!! "Come on Ma... we gotta go" ...don't let her go or reach back... put your other hand under her armpit... move towards the door... follow Angelo..."Come on Ma... we gotta go!!!"

He remembers as if it happened a few minutes ago... pulling away each finger... one at a time... "Come on Ma... we gotta go"... another finger... her wailing... "Honest, Ma, we gotta go"... all fingers free... quickly pull her hand and arm away from the casket..."We gotta go... we gotta go..."

"Please God!!! Please God!!! Don't let me do this... Please!!!"

Shit!!! Shit!!! Shit!!!... never again do I want to feel like that... NEVER... EVER... again... NEVER... "I'm sorry Ma... I'm sorry... but I gotta... we gotta"...Angelo is pulling... "We gotta go... life has gotta go on... I'm sorry Ma..."

Pg Dn

Tony thought... *Gotta be the god damn wine that puts me into this mood... gotta be the purple stains... those on the table... those in the bottom of the wine glass... those in the bottom of the wine bottle... but most of all... those in the bottom of your heart... I'm sorry Ma... Honest. I'm sorry... but we gotta go!!!....*

Pg Up

Tony was not there, but Donetta told him. When Pa came out of one of his last operations and was leaving the

'recovery room' on a hospital gurney, Donetta said he looked around and asked for Ma. When Ma stepped up beside the gurney, he reached up a little and took hold of her hand. Pa said…"I was looking for you…"

That's all he said… "I was looking for you…"

Pg Dn

… It may sound like a scriptwriter's line from a closing scene… but it wasn't. It was true. You see, Pa was the last to meet Ma… of all of her brothers and sisters in America. In those days bachelors would board, a bed, maybe one to a room… dinner and maybe a lunch. Pa got to meet all the family. He baptized Donetta and then he baptized Carmella just before he was going back to see his parents in the old country. "Pete… we got a younger sister… why don't you go and see her and meet our family in Vasto. She is a pretty little girl and is strong and healthy… everybody likes her. Why don't you go meet her?"

And he did. Pa married Ma and three months later brought her to America.

No Romeo & Juliet story, no shooting stars… no moonlight sonatas… no violins or soft music, none of that. He was in America… some opportunity… she was in Italy and it was hard times there… maybe need is better than love. They needed one another. What is better, to need and then grow to love, or to love and then seek a need… *a need*… that neither partner knows of or imagines.

Tony sat and puffed and watched the bluish gray smoke rise. He then looked down at his thighs and smirked… *did I call them pillars??? Shit, they are more like two half kegs covered in stretched denim and your stomach could be Vesuvius*!!! He lifted his legs and since he was wearing Levi denim shorts, he could easily see his socks, sneakers, and calves. Pa had no hair on his calves. Tony knew why. He remembered his father dressing or undressing, going to bed or going to work in the kitchen. It was warmer there or cooler there depending upon the season and he could put on the light too. His legs, from the knees down, were white and almost silky and, as they used to say, as smooth as a baby's ass. There was nothing else about him like ***that*** whatsoever.

Pg Up

An officer's staff vehicle drove into the hospital area and parked near the flagpole, with the red and white Red Cross flag fluttering in the spring mountain air. A line officer, a true line officer… not one from Milan… or Genoa… with family connections and no trigger time, got out and told his driver to stay put. It was obvious from the condition of his uniform that the Colonel was not coming off of the parade field, but from the mountains up by Caporetto. The field officer looked around and was about to make his way to the large tent nearby when the doctor in charge of the field hospital, and of equal rank, came out to meet him.

"Yes… he is from up the line… yes… Grazia a Dio (thank God)… the line is stabilizing… we are holding… and yes… looks like we'll continue to hold…"

But now… to the business at hand, "Doctor, I am sending down ten of my men from the demolitions squad… there were fifteen… they have been protecting our rear for the last three weeks… maybe more… blowing up trees and sometimes bridges… to slow the Austrian and Germans' advance… they haven't eaten a decent meal in more than a month and haven't bathed… they haven't rested well… if at all… and always were in sight and in range of the enemy… I want you examine them… and per l'amour de Dio (for the love of God), feed them and clean them up… can you give them uniforms?? Yes???

Good!!! Good…"

The field officer smiled. It was probably the only time he had smiled that week.

"If they are fit send them back in a day or two… they are brave men… they did their duty…" The doctor nodded his approval and understanding…"They will be coming down in a mule-pulled wagon… the same one they had used to carry the explosives and other equipment. Send them all back, please… the men, the wagon and the mule… the mule has done her job too… and all are valuable"…. He smiled again… and was about to salute the doctor… but the doctor saluted him first and said he understands.

The field officer said, "Te reingraizia." (I thank you.)

The Colonel Doctor immediately turned and left the flag pole area, seeking one of his orderlies. He found two and that was good; they had a lot of work to do. "Get two fires started outside by the rear of the tent… get three of those open ended oil drums we use in the kitchen… heat water… start filling them with hot water… get a couple of liters of kerosene… make sure you got enough wood to keep the fires going for a long time… get some blankets… at least a dozen from supply… bring them here… then go back and check for some clean, but once used, uniforms and boots" The frugal doctor buried the dead almost naked… only underwear and if they had a cross or religious medal on a chain… that's all… they didn't even need that.

"There'll be a lot of activity soon enough… tell the kitchen to have some pasta asciutto (sauceless macaroni) ready by… what time is it???… by the fifteenth hour… there is a wagon coming in from the front lines… come and get me as soon as it is here… I will be in the main tent making the rounds… keep the fire going… we're going to need more water than usual" …he lit up a Tuscan cigar and disappeared inside the main tent. The orderlies scurried about and started things going.

It was not a grand entrance, a mangy old mule, with quite a few hairless patches on its hide, pulling a squeaking old flat bed wagon… with ten very dirty and not too aromatic smelling soldiers on board. One of the orderlies raised his eyes to heaven and told his counterpart… "the mule smells better than these guys." One went to fetch the Colonel doctor.

The dirty and smelly soldiers got off of the flat bed wagon, weapons still in hand and just stood around not knowing what was going to happen. They all looked tired and drawn. The Colonel doctor came and asked, "Who is senior?"

"That would be me, Sir. Sergeant Zizzi."

"Good! Get the next senior, strip all your clothes off... give them to the orderly and climb into the oil drum... the water is warm... and the orderlies will help you in and out... I want you to soak in them for a few minutes." The Colonel doctor then put an ample amount of kerosene into each of the drums. The men stripped and placed their uniforms on the ground, the orderlies, using long sticks, picked up the clothing and carefully and gingerly placed them on the roaring fires, like it was a ceremonial sacrifice. They deposited them and soon they could smell and hear them being consumed by the small inferno.

"Once you get into the drum, I want you to close your eyes tightly pinch your nose and submerge your entire head into the water... I want you to do it at least five times... then go to the other drum that has soapy water and rinse yourself thoroughly... we've got blankets for you when you are done... I want to see each of you for an exam...", the doctor turned to an orderly and said..."Help them in and out."

And so it went, two at a time, in a primitive but effective de-lousing procedure. One of the men waiting his turn whispered to one of his companions... "I was worried... I thought these guys were cannibals when I saw the heated oil drums;" they smiled at each other.

Once the routine was established, the remaining men just stripped and threw their clothing into the fire... something about a stranger poking around with a stick and picking up what was part of you for so long and just dumping it onto an inferno... No thank you, I'll do it myself.

Part of the field, as well as parade, attire, was leggings. The leggings were about four inches wide and quite long. They were always wrapped tightly around the calves. When Tony's father took his off, he noticed most of the hair on his calves went with it. The leggings crackled with what seemed like joy as they disintegrated in the fire.

During the first phase of the de-lousing procedure... when the occupant was pinching his nose and dunking, an orderly would skim off the top of the kerosene with a dust pan. He would pick and skim off the body lice that rose to the top of the water. He would occasionally add a tub, or more, of warm water.

Pg Dn

Tony looked at his keg-leg thighs and mountainous stomach and wondered if he could ever get into an oil drum. He looked at his hands; Pa had good hands... Ma used to say "Mano d'ora." (Hands of gold.)

He sipped his wine and wished he had known his father better... and wished he had been a better son. *Whadda guy!!!* He really and truly wished he had known him better.

All Hold Hands... and Fall Down

Tony was suddenly antsy. He had been happy telling and reliving the incidents in this narrative and well within the confines of his own brain, in his head, miles away from reality or as close to it as the Page Up button. But after again admitting his perceived failings as a son, something left him. That little spark... the follow-up of memories... the countless stories he heard... the urgency to tell... the urgency to share, is no longer as vivid or as vital.

In his heart he knew, however, that he had to finish the telling of Uncle Joe and Uncle Dan and his poor Enzo... *whadda bad break for dat young kid*!!! The other men in his life he knew and grew to love, but the other one, Enzo, he whom he never met only had heard of. They were all so real, so very real and very human. At that moment, Tony felt that he understood that the one man, he whom he never met, meant the most. *It is not gunna be wine tonight… naw… sumptin stronger… sumptin…* he opened the bottom right hand drawer… the double one that was about twelve to fifteen inches high. *Boy!! It's heavy…* pulled it open and rummaged around a couple of old magazines, newspapers… maybe a couple of files and large envelopes and found what he was looking for.

He got up and went to the bathroom and came back with a pink plastic cup that was used for the mouthwash. He rinsed it and thought, with his East Utica attitude and sarcasm… *Yeah!!! That's gunna help a lot!!!* He took his hidden bottle of Wild Turkey, filled his mouth-washing cup more than half full with the whiskey, raised it to eye level… then about another inch or two higher… to his hairline level… and… *to the four men in his thoughts…* he simply said… *Saluti…*

Pg Up

… Uncle Joe was in the hospital… on the fifth floor… April 1965… he was pretty sick. Tony's wife had delivered his first son on the third floor in an entirely different section of the hospital at about the same time.

Tony would stop up to the fifth floor, once in a while, to go chat with Uncle Joe, a rotund old man of eighty three, long widowed, who saw so much and remembered so much. They were pleasant visits for both, at least Tony thought so!

In time, Tony took home his first son… and mother… and child… did well. Uncle Joe overcame his current medical problems and was released. They, Tony and Uncle Joe, met again in the late spring at Zia Grazia and Uncle Dan's apartment. Uncle Joe in an old wrinkled suit, shirt and tie, was sitting by the cupboard, which had two fairly large swinging cupboard doors in the upper half, that were divided into twelve small, glass plates, six on each door. There were two swinging wood doors on the lower portion that opened into a shelved area for pots and pans and kettles.

What's wrong? What's wrong?" She turned to her mother who just shrugged her shoulders but was starting to cry too. "PA!!! PA!!! What is the matter???"

He was openly weeping now, he answered… but his words were much too slurred to understand. He was trying to say… *Sun a ma beach… I can't move my arm and hand to pick up the sun a ma bitchen spoon… son of a bitch… what is wrong with me??? Bastardia!* He reached over with his left arm and tried to lift his other hand. Donetta and Zia Grazia knew then what was wrong.

They all now wept and she told her father, "It's all right Pa it's all right, I'll help you." And she did.

A little bit later, three strong men came over to Zia Grazia's apartment, two of her grandsons and one of her nephews. They sat Uncle Dan in the same chair that Uncle Joe sat in when he gave Tony the blue envelope with five dollars in it, and they steered and jockeyed him around and made it to the top of the staircase. Once there, two of them stepped down on to the stairs, took a firm hold on the back legs of the chair and started the descent. The other man lifted and supported the back of the chair. There were sixteen steps to descend, they had to cross a small hallway and then out into the driveway.

They decided it would be easier to lay him in the back of a bakery truck. They took him to the General Hospital on South and Mohawk Streets. He had long ago stopped weeping.

Tony was sorry he was not there to help, he would have been honored.

That right hand, once so mighty, that literally destroyed three men from Yonkers, so many years ago in a warm bakery but on a very cold February morning… that one final day… that hand… could not pick up a tablespoon so that he could eat some good soup. He passed on, picturing a bowl of thick wedding soup… the aroma of the soup and his daughter's and his wife's anxious, but loving looks.

Pg Dn

Tony has to remind himself that neither Ma or Pa, Zia Grazia or Uncle Dan, Zia Lucia, none of them were in l'America when Enzo committed that grievous sin. Tony had heard the story from Zia Grazia and Ma... and *Ma sez so... so it's gotta be true!!!*

Ma told the story of the one, the one that Tony, if he allowed himself to, could understand the most.

Pg Up

Enzo took some money from the cigar box, not all of it, but some. Lot of tens and twenties were there to pay Mr. Griffin the flour man. He walked the twelve blocks to Union Station, purchased a one way ticket to *la Citta*, or *Nueva Yorka*, as the old timers would say it, and eventually boarded a train and went seeking L'America.

The City was not kind to him. Full of so many strangers... no family... no piasanos... people with no love in their hearts... but worse... nobody cared. He found jobs here and there, was cheated more than once, robbed in a flop house. Lucky he didn't keep all his money in one spot. Soon, he was out of money... soon, he was always so cold... soon, nobody wanted a strong young man to lift and move and pull stuff... soon, they would neglect to put the blanket over his eyes when he emerged into the daylight.

One day he returned to the flop house, his few possessions were on the front stoop and his bed given to another. He went to the park. He had to gather his thoughts; there was a toilet in the park and some benches and a kind of pavilion built for when it rained. He stayed there, sleeping on park benches, sometimes covering himself with old newspapers, sometimes pulling up old weeds and making a mattress of them under a park bench and then sleeping on them. *Sta attenda per le polizia!!!* Be careful of the police, with all those brass buttons down the front of their coats.

One particular morning, he was not feeling good, it

was getting cold. It had rained all night. Everything around him was wet; he shivered, but could not get warm. The laths of the park bench, above his head and body, allowed the cold October rain to fall on him. It chilled him; his nose and face were very close to the earth. He smelled it, but then had to cough. It was a barking cough and his entire body shuddered. *Gotta get warm… gotta get warm…*

He opened his eyes for a moment and saw the shoes of a police man very near his face. He soon felt the poke of the policeman's billy club at his knee. "Come on… come on, ya bum, get up and get out of 'ear… come on!!!"

With super human effort Enzo got up, but as soon as he was up, he fell into the park bench and rolled his head. The police officer, the son of a second generation Irishman, easily recognized fatigue and exhaustion when he saw it. "Whattsa madder, kid, you sick or sumptin?" Enzo tried to answer in Italian, but only managed to flop over onto the bench seat. Officer Cahill looked at him and then quickly looked around.

The Gods finally looked down upon this wretched cold and freezing kid and said, "Let's give him a break!!!" Two Italian Franciscan Nuns just happen to be walking in the park in their black and white habits, carrying and sharing a black umbrella. Cahill, a product of the early parochial school system, called out, "Sisters… Sisters… could you come here for a second?" They came, side by side… the Nuns always traveled in pairs, and Cahill continued… "this kid looks like he is pretty sick and if I run him in, he'll only be put into a corner and eventually they'll throw him out of the precinct… do ya think you can get him help??? He is Italian… I heard him say something a few minutes ago in Italian."

The Gods of Contentment and Happiness still continued to listen and soon smiled again upon this wretched soul. "Yes!!! …of course… of course… Sister Mary Elvira… go, run to St. Rocco and ask for Father Carmine and bring him here…" "Will you be all right, Mother Superior???" "Yes, of course... take the umbrella…" "But it is raining…" "Don't worry… if it rains harder I'll wait under that pavilion… now hurry!!!" "But Mother…" "Go!! Go!!"

Who said there is NO GOD? Father Carmine met Father Marcagono at a communion breakfast last week and found out he was transferred from Utica and after talking... or trying to talk to Enzo discovered Enzo lived in Utica. He called the old priest from Utica, who smoked Tuscan cigars and liked to bet on the ponies.

Cold and shivering, Enzo was put up in the church basement, by the boiler, they set up a little cot there to keep him warm and they eventually made contact with Utica. "Yes they knew an Enzo from St. Anthony's (still just a basement parish)… Yes they knew the family… Yes… his brother and a Mr. Sabitano, from the bank would come down to get him… Yes!!! Yes!!! He is all right… he is a little mixed up… not a criminal… Yes, Thursday afternoon in Sheepheads Bay Brooklyn…"

They brought Enzo back to Utica, the gentle and considerate and kind Mr. Sabitano and Enzo's older brother… who should have offered him more kindness in the past. Enzo was very weak and could

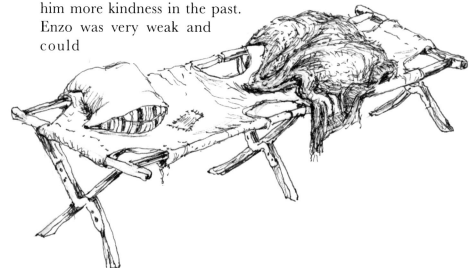

not lift and move hundred pound bags of flour, or back up Luigi Farnia when he didn't show up for work... or drive the family to the Forest Park and take the truck down to Norwich. No, he could not do that, any of that, anymore.

He was sick.

Uncle Joe brought him home. He slept with young Michael for a time, but his coughing and gagging kept him up, so adjustments were made. Uncle Joe's wife was never very comfortable with Enzo back in the house. All she could think about was the open mouth of that steamer trunk, exposing its bowels to mankind and the contents of the Dutch Master Cigar box. And poor Uncle Joe, whenever he saw Enzo would only think of his shattered dreams and his mountains of hope. For the longest time, Uncle Joe's eyes would fill up when he thought of that young man... his younger brother.

His condition worsened and soon it was decided to either send him to Broad Acres or Rome State Hospital. Tony never knew which. The boy who had grown a mustache to look older and more attractive to young girls and hoping for a full and wonderful new life in l'America, died in the hospital.

His last thoughts in this life, were of his nose snuggling into the white, bleached clean bed sheets and pillow-cases... His thoughts were only of wanting to come to "Amerika", to become a man, to make a thousand dreams come true!

L'Merica! L'Merica!

Epilogue

The Gorillas

Pg Dn

Something way back, way, way back, in Tony's memory bank would occasionally creep into his thoughts and he could not, for some unknown reason, tie it all together and make a true memory of it all. It was like something on the other side of bluish-gray cigar smoke, or, like something behind a veil in a poorly lit room, just a little too far away to distinguish. To Tony, the memory was neither pleasant nor unpleasant, but consistent in its reoccurrence. It must have been something he heard, or read, or saw in the movies or on TV; the scene certainly was never seen by him with his own two eyes; like they used to say, 'every once in a while', the scene would be revealed to him.

It was about gorillas. A band or group of gorillas in the wild. *Whaddya call a group of gorillas... a commune... a herd... a pack... a tribe... what??? Guess you can call 'em anything you want, but don't call 'em a family... anything but a family. Animals do not have immortal souls.*

As he recalls, a group of gorillas suddenly faced a serious threat. A force outside their little secure world placed them all in danger. The setting is on a barren hillside with a tree line over the crest of the hill. A small creek ran at the base of the hill and from this creek their adversaries approached.

The alarm sounded.

The mothers of the group quickly gathered their infants, clutched them to their breasts, close to their hearts and made straight for the tree line at the top of the hill. When they got there, they turned and looked down, facing the adversaries, ready to fight. They still clutched their off-spring tightly, still very close to their hearts. The matriarchs raced to the bottom of the hill, swung their free arms violently, threateningly, at the danger below.

The younger females and males followed the matri-archs up the slope. When the matriarchs stopped and turned, they did too. The young females quickly formed a line a few feet between the mothers and the lurk-ing danger. They too yelled their threats. The younger males did the same thing, only they formed their defense line about two paces in front of the young females. The infants clung to their mothers, wide eyed and some-what confused by all the commotion and yelling. But in their innocence, they felt safe and secure, pressed to their mother's breast and smelling her scent.

The older gorillas, the three or four young bulls, formed their defense line mid-way on the slope, as they too faced the adversaries. Slightly off their hams, they leaned forward, their long arms out to the front of them barely touching the earth. We are ready!

The alpha male, now slightly gray with age and maybe a half step slower on the run, but still as strong in the shoulders and arms as he ever was, placed himself between the young bulls and the lurking danger. He roared and beat his chest loudly, announcing to all: *this is mine... it is ours... it is theirs... not yours... go away... or fight all of us.*

The alpha male stood out there unafraid and willing to die for what was his, as well as, theirs. Behind him, in tiers, was the reason, the support and the love... and the babies!

What is the difference between instincts of survival and immortality? *But we call them anything... anything... but family.*

The Blue Bird of East Utica

In that old "Kung Fu" television series, someone asks the Chinese monk, "who is the greatest person on earth?" The sage had a one word reply (and in lower case, mind you) it was simply, "Nobody." And the Gospel tells us, "Those who serve are the greatest among you."

First light came early; it was the month of May. Tony awoke, blinked a few times and got oriented... the drapes, the ceiling fan, the large framed collage of photographs and snapshots his wife made up for him... a Father's Day gift... way back when. He rubbed his face into his special pillow... this week with the blue pillow case, blinked again and listened. *Quiet!!!*

His first thought of that day was not an original thought, but a memory of sitting out in the enclosed porch yesterday. He, with his Tuscan cigar and a glass of Bolla Chianti, rocking in one of those one seat lounge chairs that came with the over priced lawn set (two rockers with armrests and four straight backed, conventional chairs), rocking slowly back and forth, contented. His eldest son was seated in the two-seated glider, also a piece of the over priced, matching lawn furniture set. A peaceful quiet afternoon.

Down by the arbor, a small, about twenty or so inches tall, statue of Saint Francis of Assisi stood guard over Caesar's final resting place. Caesar, that little multi colored beagle that Tony often told his friends and relatives helped him raise his three kids. They had him more than seventeen years. "Ole' Caesar" was placed to rest in a circular slightly mounded grave. Tony and his kids placed field stones around the circumference of the grave and over the past ten years planted marigolds and pansies on the mound, stuff like that. Some friends mentioned the grave might be against township ordinances, which may or may not be true, but Tony was determined that Caesar should rest on their property… ordinance or not. Tony never lost that East Utica attitude… *who sez I can't?? Nobody who was anybody said anything to me 'bout not doing it… if he had to… I'd rather beg forgiveness than ask permission...* and besides… *who the hell died and left you boss?*

The statue of St. Francis of Assissi had been purchased, blessed and stationed nearby, *because ma sez Santo Francisco was the patron saint of animals.* Plus, Tony believes and feels that his little beagle is happy there. One Saturday afternoon, long ago, Tony and the grandkids put a couple of coats of white enamel outdoor paint on the statue. The kids, naturally, made a mess. Tony's wife and daughter, naturally, went bananas. Much later, after the kids were gone and the paint dried, Tony painted the three birds on the statue; one on St. Francis' shoulder, another on his forearm and the last one by his feet. Tony painted them a sky blue. The kids did as good a job as Pops did.

When Tony bought the birdbath a couple of years back, he had originally wanted to place it down by the arbor and the grave. His wife talked him out of it; she thought it would be much better by the screened in porch where and when the occasion arose, he could watch the birds come in and drink and sometime even splash around in the bowl and bathe. Tony admits, *when you are right you are right…* and in this case she was right on the money. *She was right!*

So, the birdbath was placed on a small concrete pedestal near the screened in porch and the grave remained by the arbor on the back lot. If you sat in Tony's chair and looked southwest you would be able to see all four; the birdbath, the grave, the arbor and the fig tree. A long way from Catherine Street… *dat's fur sure!*

Anyway, yesterday afternoon Tony was pleasantly surprised and immediately became mesmerized by the quick and accurate landing of a bluebird on the outer rim of the birdbath. He had seen these bluebirds for the first time last summer and never dreamed that they would come to drink and bathe... *Wow, this is great, look at 'em!*

"Pete... Pete..." he whispered "...Look!! Look!!... its one of those blue birds I told you about"... Peter saw the bird, and his eyes widened and his lower jaw dropped a bit. They both stared at the bird, Tony half holding his breath for fear it might take flight, but it didn't. The bird drank from the perch on the rim of the birdbath and then suddenly jumped right into the center and half flapped his wings. He created a tempest in the center of the shallow bath.

What a beautiful sight. Last year was the first time Tony saw, or at least, truly recognized seeing, an honest to God living bluebird. He was over seventy years old, "it's about time!" He knew his son was equally awed by the sight, too.

The bird hopped back up again on to the rim of the birdbath... looked quickly around... all three-hundred and sixty degrees... *and in the blink of a young girl's eye* (Springsteen) was gone. Father and son looked at one another and smiled; Tony added, "How about that!!!" This bluebird, like the one last year, had an orangish breast like a robin, but was distinct in the almost flourescent hue of its wings. *That baby was no robin!!!* Tony's limited research lead him to believe it was a Northeastern Bluebird of the 'whatever it is called' species. Best he could tell from the bird book he got three years ago and that stays on the table on the back screened in porch, or up until the kids come anyway.

That is what was going through Tony's mind, with his eyes closed but not sleeping anymore. He heard the garbage truck rumble up... that distinct tinkling of the recyclable tub... the motor roared again and the sound faded away.

He opened his eyes and again saw the blue pillow-case under his cheek and slowly let his eyelids drop down again and he returned to his comfortable darkness.

Who is the greatest person in the world?? Those who serve or nobody? I am far... very far... from being great, probably much closer to being nobody... but I know one thing... I watched a bluebird drink and flutter around in my birdbath at my home... in my back yard... by the arbor and the fig tree and the pear tree and everything else back there, and... I thank God for being the luckiest. It is a long way from 912 Catherine Street. And God, please bless East Utica, with or without bluebirds.

As Right As Rain

Rain falls from the heavens pure and sweet... palpable... but on its voyage to sea level, it gathers the seeds of its destruction and once at sea level, it joins the flood and becomes impure... not palatable. The ocean water is and will remain unpalatable. Salty, like human blood and tears. Then, something happens and any fifth grader can easily explain, some of the sea water evaporates, forms clouds that drift over land and sea and the rains again fall from the heavens... again pure... and... sweet... and palatable water.

Somewhere there is an old man seated in an old urine-stained... in a good, solid rocking chair. It is not a pretty picture, but, he and it were not always that way. Both have seen much better days. The rocker remains solid, well built, sturdy at the joints and crucial points; and the old man remains somewhat solid and well built and sturdy, but in a different way. His thoughts go, return and go again, and return again and are often of the very young, the children in his family. A part of them carry some of his chromosomes. He is happy and content... *Hail Mary, full of grace... Oh my Jesus forgive us our sins, save us from the fires of hell... a peaceful death, O Lord... a peaceful death... like St. Joseph, please!*

Tony recalled a conversation with Ma just a couple of years before she passed on. Ma had left the old brown-stone tenement house on Catherine Street and relocated to another nearby neighborhood. It was better for all the obvious urban reasons and had the extra bonus of having two nieces and a grandniece living on the same block. It was a second floor apartment in a frame building owned by one of her nieces, who resided on the first floor front and had done so for a number of years, raising her children and burying her husband. The apartment had only three rooms and a large bathroom with a tub and a side porch. One of the rooms was kind of small; the other was larger than she had ever been used to. The kitchen, finally, was more square than rectangular, unlike the one on Catherine Street and had two windows that faced outward to the porch. A change for the better... for sure!! But what made the apartment close to being like heaven, was the fact that the house had a furnace and all the rooms had a furnace register... "all the rooms!"

In, what turned out to be her final living space, she was happy, finding friends and sometimes relatives to take her to mass at Saint Anthony's every morning except Saturdays. On Saturdays, they went to the eight o'clock mass at St. Stan's and sometimes after mass, they would go to a Mac Donalds for breakfast. Each party would treat in rotation. It was surprising how inexpensive the total bill was when it was Ma's turn to pay. God bless those East Uticans, God bless them all.

In the quiet peacefulness, warmth and security of her warm apartment one cold November day, Tony asked Ma, "Ma, are you afraid of dying?"

Her answer took him aback. Ma and her church, her novenas, her daily trek up to the altar to receive the Host, the procession in the street following the saints, her zillion and zillion daily (if not more) recitals of the Holy Rosaries, the tears that fell from her eyes when she heard the Passion week's Gospels... all that and more flashed through Tony's mind when he heard her reply.

Pg Up

Then another scene popped into his head, back, way back, during the war, Tony came home from the school yard early, opened the yellow screen door and walked into the kitchen... thinking, *where's Ma?*...on his way to the boys' bedroom to hang up his hat, he glanced at Ma and Pa's bedroom door, it was ajar.

Oh, so there she is!! He was about to push the door fully open and announce his arrival home, but something stopped him. Ma was kneeling at the bed saying the rosaries in a semi dark room, the shades were drawn to keep the flat cool on this Indian summer day, and was so engrossed she had not heard her youngest son come home.

He saw in her profile a stream of tears running from her eye, past her nose and down over her cheek. The tears looked silvery in the darkened room, catching and reflecting what little light was in the room. Tony reached for the door knob, caught it and gently and quietly pulled it back to its original position.

He took two steps back, confused and for some unbeknownst reason, to him anyway, he was very, very sad. To this day, Tony cannot look at that painting of Christ in the Garden of Gethsemane… from the pulpit the priest would tell the kids *He sweated blood…* and not relive that silent moment.

Tony left the flat, quietly closed the yellow screen door, went down the rear staircase and sat on the back alley stoop… alone. He sat there a long, long time.

Pg Dn

And this woman… the holiest you will ever meet in two lifetimes… quickly and confidently answered Tony's question.

"Yes, of course, I am afraid to die… Gesu Himself was afraid."

The rocker has a urine stain in its finish… and rain water from the sky is always palatable.

Glossary of Adages

From Abruzzi and La Puglia

Three most potent things in the world

La vucca (the mouth)
Lu ventu (the wind)
e (and)
Quelli che non sa niente (those who know nothing)

The three coldest things on Earth
u nasu du cane (the nose of the dog)
U calcagno du monacu (the heel of a monk)
U culu da femmina (the ass of a woman)

Ricco quando voglia… u povero quando possa
The rich when they want… the poor when they can

S' è sposa la regina?
Did the queen get married?

Manga aiuto al cervello
His brain does not help him

Quando metti gli sensi?
When are you going to get some sense?
Quando scatti?
When you burst?

Ogni casa ha na croce
Every house has a cross

Sette ha fatto a mammata... Ma tu sei a più bella
Your mother made seven... but... you... you are the most
beautiful

Sempre sai dove se nato... ma nessuno sa dove se mori
You'll always know where you were born... but you'll
never know where
you'll die

Chiudere l'occhi e bevi l'aceto
Close your eyes and drink the vinegar

Fa beni e scorda
Do good and forget it
Fa mali e ricorda
Do bad and remember

Quello che mancu nasci... non mori
Those who are not born don't die

Uno per me, uno per te, e uno per il figlio du Re
One for me, one for you and on for the son of the king

A volpe cambia la pelle, ma non il vizio
A fox will change his fur, but not his habits

Che pesce si?
What kind of fish are you?

Hai fatto na buca na l'acqua
You made a hole in the water

Cu a testa fai tutto
In your head you do everything